# THE BASICS
# BUSINESS
# COMMUNICATION

Patricia Merrier
University of Minnesota Duluth
Duluth, Minnesota

**THOMSON**

Australia · Brazil · Canada · Mexico · Singapore · Spain · United Kingdom · United States

SOUTH-WESTERN

The Basics: Business Communication, 3e
Patricia Merrier

**VP/Editorial Director:**
Jack W. Calhoun

**VP/Editor-in-Chief:**
Karen Schmohe

**Acquisitions Editor:**
Jane Phelan

**Developmental Editor:**
Penny Shank

**Production Editor:**
Darrell E. Frye

**Marketing Manager:**
Valerie A. Lauer

**Manufacturing Coordinator:**
Kevin Kluck

**Compositor:**
Cadmus Inc.

**Production Manager:**
Graphic World Inc.

**Consulting Editor:**
Elaine Langlois

**Printer:**
Edwards Brothers

**Art Director:**
Stacy Jenkins Shirley

**Cover and Internal Designer:**
Lou Ann Thesing

**Cover Images:**
© Getty Images

**Asia (including India)**
Thomson Learning
5 Shenton Way
#01-01 UIC Building
Singapore 068808

**Australia/New Zealand**
Thomson Learning Australia
102 Dodds Street
Southbank, Victoria 3006
Australia

**Canada**
Thomson Nelson
1120 Birchmount Road
Toronto, Ontario
M1K 5G4
Canada

**Latin America**
Thomson Learning
Seneca, 53
Colonia Polanco
11560 Mexico
D. F. Mexico

**UK/Europe/Middle East/Africa**
Thomson Learning
High Holborn House
50/51 Bedford Row
London WC1R 4LR
United Kingdom

**Spain (including Portugal)**
Thomson Paraninfo
Calle Magallanes, 25
28015 Madrid, Spain

# CONTENTS

# PREFACE

You are about to explore a dynamic and important area of your business program. Clear, accurate, timely written communication is critical to the success of both you and the organization for which you work.

## Organization

*The Basics: Business Communication* is designed to help you refine your writing skills and adapt them to business situations. The text-workbook contains seven chapters:

- Chapter 1 introduces you to the communication process, including the characteristics of business messages and the barriers that interfere with effective communication.

- Chapter 2 takes you through the mental and physical processes of planning business messages.

- Chapter 3 discusses the 4Cs of business communication and their importance in business writing.

- Chapters 4 through 6 present and let you apply the strategies used when writing positive, neutral, negative, and persuasive messages.

- Chapter 7 addresses the process of preparing application letters, résumés, and other employment communications, as well as special business messages.

## Special Features

*The Basics: Business Communication* is more than a textbook. It is a practical, results-oriented tool with the following features designed to help you write effective business messages:

- The **Thinking it Through** features in each chapter challenge you to know what items to include in a message as well as why and how to include them.

- **Thinking it Through solutions**, provided at the end of the book, let you verify your understanding of one section before you begin another section.

- **Examples** clarify and reinforce chapter concepts.

- **Message-writing activities** cover both business and personal-business situations.

- **Margin notes and quotations** help you learn and recall important concepts.

- **Workplace Connections** offer tips for succeeding on the job and improving your written communications.

- **E-mail and Internet** activities help you develop skills associated with using technology in business communication.

- **Communication Comment** features and cartoons add realism and humor to your study of business communication.

- **Chapter summaries** reinforce the principles covered in each chapter.

- **Chapter applications** allow you to put what you have learned to work using your critical thinking, composition, proofreading, and teamwork skills.

- *The Basics: Business Communication* **website** at **http://merrier.swlearning.com** offers additional activities, crossword puzzles that reinforce chapter vocabulary, links to useful sites, and other helpful materials.

- **Appendixes** provide common letter and memo formats, a list of editing symbols, and a guide to frequently confused/misused words.

## Icons

*The Basics: Business Communication* uses icons to help you quickly identify some of its special features:

### Chart of Icons

| Icon | Explanation |
|------|-------------|
| | The Internet icon marks activities in which you may practice your online computer skills. |
| | The e-mail icon indicates activities to be completed using e-mail. |

## The Series

*The Basics: Business Communication* may be used as a stand-alone resource or in conjunction with **The Basics Series**, a series of text-workbooks that helps you master the communication skills needed in the workplace. The other books in the series are *The Basics: English*, *The Basics: Writing*, *The Basics: Employment Communication*, *The Basics: Speech Communication*, and *The Basics: Proofreading*.

## Acknowledgments

Thanks are extended to the following individuals for reviewing *The Basics: Business Communication* and for offering suggestions for revision:

**Deann K. Blankenship,** Kaw Area Technical School, Topeka, KS

**Nancy Stewart,** Cisco Junior College, Cisco, TX

**Sherry Todd,** Owensboro High School, Owensboro, KY

This text acquaints you with the principles and processes necessary to communicate well. With study and practice, YOU can write effective business messages. Enjoy your study. Work hard. Succeed.

*Patricia Merrier*

# Understanding the Communication Process

**1**

The National Association of Colleges and Employers (NACE) annually surveys employers to determine the job outlook for college graduates. The NACE report includes information about what employers look for in job candidates. The results of this survey consistently show communication (verbal and written) ranking *first* in the list of qualities/skills employers want—ahead of assets such as honesty/integrity and computer skills. Ironically, communication is also among the skills employers say new graduates lack.

## COMMUNICATION IN THE WORKPLACE

Communication is the heart of every organization. Whether the organization is a family, a social or professional society, a not-for-profit entity, or a for-profit business, its members must interact—*communicate*. Good reading, writing, speaking, and listening skills are essential to accomplishing tasks and achieving goals.

"Wait," you say. "I've been communicating my whole life. What's different about this?"

The difference is that now you'll be focusing on *workplace* communication. You'll be asked to sharpen your skills and to apply them in new and different situations. Some of your communication efforts will be individual ones; others will be collaborative. In either case, you'll perform them in a professional manner. Everything you do will relate to an objective or a goal. Your ability to communicate will mean success for you and your employer.

## Why Communication Skills Are Important to You

You're enrolled in a postsecondary school program because you want to develop the skills needed to get a job and build a career. Communication is certainly one of those skills. As you work to

### LEARNING OBJECTIVES

- Be aware of the role communication plays in the workplace.
- Understand the communication process.
- Identify the characteristics of business messages.
- Recognize communication barriers and identify ways to minimize them.

*Employees and organizations need to communicate to succeed.*

build a successful career, you'll find that effective communication will be important in the following three ways:

1. **You must communicate to get your job.** You'll use your communication skills to prepare your application letter and résumé and to sell yourself during an interview.

2. **You must communicate to do your job effectively.** Regardless of the position you hold, you will interact with colleagues, supervisors, clients, customers, and/or representatives of other organizations. Sharing data, preparing reports, collaborating on projects, and providing good customer service all require strong communication skills.

3. **You must communicate to advance in your career.** Good communication skills get noticed and are often a factor in deciding who gets promoted. In addition, employers look for employees who can think, solve problems, and communicate their ideas for improving products and procedures. Showing you are interested in the long-term success of the organization will make you one of its valued and promoted members.

## Why Employers Seek Workers Who Communicate Well

You needn't look further than the classified ads in your local newspaper to know that employers want to hire people who have good communication skills. The ability to communicate effectively is listed as a desirable qualification in many classified ads. Why?

Effective communication at all levels is essential for an organization to succeed. If you think for a moment about the many ways in which an organization relies on communication, you will see that this is so. In addition, organizations today face certain challenges that call for excellent communication skills:

1. **The workplace is highly specialized.** Workers may not understand one another's technical vocabulary. Therefore, they must work hard to ensure that their messages are clear and complete.

2. **The workplace is diverse.** The global nature of business and the diversity of the domestic workforce mean that employees must consider the demographic characteristics of those with whom they communicate. Age, gender, disabilities, and race/ethnicity are among the factors to be recognized and respected.

3. **The workplace relies on technology.** Technology affects the type and speed of our communications. Workers must know how and when to use technology to help them communicate.

*" During the interview itself, I am highly sensitive to the relative strength or weakness of the individual's communication skills. It is essential for the candidate to be able to communicate clearly. "*

**-Elaine Swope, Director of Human Resources, Specialty Care Network**

Today's businesses face certain challenges:

■ Specialization

■ Diversity

■ Technology

*Chapter 1: Understanding the Communication Process*

## Valuing Communication

List three ways in which communication affects the job you currently have or the job you expect to hold after completing your educational program. Be specific.

1.

2.

3.

## The Focus of this Book

Although all types of communication are important in the workplace, this text will focus on written communication. You'll become acquainted with the kinds of written communication you can expect to use on the job. In addition, you'll learn and practice techniques designed to help you produce effective messages. Ready? Let's begin!

# COMMUNICATION CHARACTERISTICS

When asked to describe a friend, you will probably provide information about the person's physical characteristics (height, hair color, weight) and aspects of the person's character (honesty, loyalty, generosity). The same approach can be used when describing communication; the only difference is in the terms used. *Mode*, *destination*, *flow*, and *style* are among the terms used to describe the features of communication.

## Mode

The **mode** is the method that people use to communicate. Sometimes it is words; sometimes it is actions. When communication is with words, its mode is **verbal**. Verbal communication may be spoken or written. Do not confuse verbal communication with oral communication, which is always spoken. Speeches, introductions, conversations, letters, memos, e-mail, and reports are examples of verbal communication. A communication's mode is **nonverbal** when it occurs through actions or appearance. Handshakes, smiles, and frowns are examples of nonverbal communication. The format of a letter or report illustrates nonverbal communication associated with written messages. A letter positioned unattractively on the page conveys a negative message; a neatly formatted report conveys a positive message.

*Verbal communication may be spoken or written.*

## Destination

The **destination** is the target audience. Business communication can be directed to *internal* or *external* receivers. **Internal** communication occurs when workers within an organization communicate with one another. A memo announcing a change in a personnel policy or an e-mail containing the agenda for a budget meeting is an example of internal communication. **External** communication occurs when employees send messages to people who do not belong to the organization. A letter to a customer explaining that an order has been delayed or an air quality report submitted to a state agency is an external communication.

## Flow

**Flow** is the path communication takes or the direction in which it is sent. Communication can flow vertically, horizontally, or diagonally within the workplace.

Messages can flow vertically, horizontally, or diagonally within an organization.

### VERTICAL COMMUNICATION.

**Vertical communication** moves between individuals at different organizational levels. Sometimes messages are sent from the CEO to all employees within an organization or from a vice president to all employees in his or her area only. Generally, though, vertical communication follows the "chain of command," the reporting lines reflected on an organizational chart. This means that a manager will send messages *downward* to those he or she supervises. Similarly, a worker will send messages *upward* to the person to whom he or she reports.

For organizations to be successful, the vertical lines of communication must be open. Employees want to know what is happening within their organization and why it is happening. They also want to know that their ideas and suggestions are welcomed and valued. Reports, announcements, newsletters, policy statements, and meetings all facilitate the kind of information exchange that keeps morale high and rumors and gossip to a minimum.

### HORIZONTAL COMMUNICATION.

**Horizontal communication** flows between or among peers (employees at the same organizational level). Messages that flow horizontally typically involve the exchange of data or information needed to accomplish routine tasks. The information can be shared through memos, e-mail, or reports; during face-to-face conversations; or via telephone. The senders and receivers can be in the same department or in different units. The common bond is their need to cooperate.

### DIAGONAL COMMUNICATION.

**Diagonal communication** is exchanged between people who work in different units and at different levels within an organization. These messages facilitate the work of

## WORKPLACE CONNECTION

Teams are the norm in business today, and effective interpersonal communication (e.g., listening, speaking, resolving conflicts, negotiating) is essential to both team membership and team leadership.

*Chapter 1: Understanding the Communication Process*

committees, teams, and task forces created to solve problems or complete projects.

## Style

Regardless of their destination or flow, messages have one of two styles—*formal* or *informal*. **Formal** communications use traditional formats. **Informal** communications are more free-flowing and relaxed. Letters, for example, will use the receiver's street mailing address; memos and e-mail will not. A formal written report will have a title page and a table of contents; an informal written report will not.

Formal style does not require formal language. In most cases, business writing should be conversational, neither too stiff nor too casual.

## Other Features

Business communications should be both ethical and legal. An **ethical message** meets the unwritten moral expectations of society. Meeting these standards is a matter of trust and integrity. When the expectations are not met, society's trust is violated and the violator's integrity is questioned. If repeated violations occur, society responds by enacting laws designed to enforce its ethical standards. Consumer protection laws, for example, were enacted to ensure fair treatment in interactions between buyers and sellers. A **legal message** meets the requirements of any laws (local, state, national, or international) that apply to the contents.

© 2004 Ted Goff

"I was referring to May, 2030, when I promised a May 30 product launch."

## WORKPLACE CONNECTION

Ethical standards vary by person, organization, and culture. Set high standards for yourself, maintain the high standards of your employer, and recognize and respect differences among cultures.

Determining what is ethical and legal and what is not can be challenging because of differences among governments, cultures, organizations, and individuals. Bribery (giving someone money or gifts to do something, often something dishonest) and embezzlement (stealing money or property in violation of a trust) illustrate those differences.

- In the United States, bribing a public official is illegal. In some other countries, however, bribes are expected. If a U.S. business representative gives money to an official in one of these countries, has he or she violated a law? Behaved unethically?

- In the United States, it is illegal for employees to embezzle money from their employers. Is it unethical, though, for a worker to use an organization's computer for personal activities such as keying a paper for school?

Employees have an obligation to know and adhere to the laws and codes of ethics that apply to their work.

## [THINKING IT THROUGH 1-2]

## Exploring Ethics

Some people believe the term *business ethics* is an oxymoron (a term in which the two words have contradictory meanings). Do you agree? Why or why not?

*Communication is a cyclical process.*

# THE WRITTEN COMMUNICATION PROCESS

Every written communication involves a **sender** and a **receiver**. The sender initiates the communication process, because he or she has an idea or some information to share with the receiver. The sender **encodes** (puts into words) and **transmits** (sends) the message via a **channel** (paper or electronic). The receiver then **decodes** (reads and interprets) the message and gives **feedback** to the sender. The process may be completed in one cycle, or it may be repeated several times. One cycle of the communication process is shown in Figure 1-1.

**Figure 1-1**
The Communication Process

The communication process seems simple. When it succeeds, the sender and receiver understand each other. In some cases, though, problems hamper or destroy the ability to achieve this goal. These problems are called **barriers**. Effective communicators recognize potential barriers in the process and work to minimize or eliminate them.

# BARRIERS TO COMMUNICATION

Barriers can occur at any point in the communication process. The most common written communication barriers are described in the following paragraphs.

## Poor Word Choice

The English language contains hundreds of thousands of words, and no person has command of them all. Instead, each individual develops two sets of vocabulary—a use vocabulary and a recognition vocabulary. The **use vocabulary** consists of words the individual regularly reads, hears, and/or writes. They are words he or she uses with confidence. The **recognition vocabulary** consists of words for which meaning can be derived from context. Word choice may become a barrier when the words the sender uses are not in the use or recognition vocabulary of the receiver. The relationship among user vocabulary, recognition vocabulary, and total words is shown in Figure 1-2.

_Executives say that 14 percent of each workweek is wasted because of poor communication— seven weeks each year._

**-Based on survey by OfficeTeam; reported in "Failure to Communicate Costly for Companies," by Stephanie Armour**

*Barriers impede the communication process.*

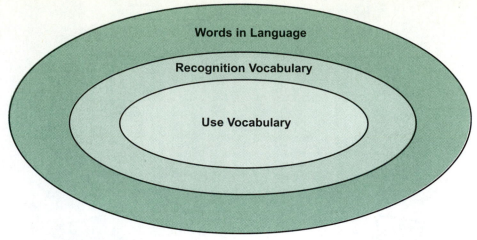

### Figure 1-2
Relationship of Vocabulary Levels

Word choice typically arises as a communication barrier when senders write to impress rather than to express and when they rely too heavily on **jargon** (specialized, work-related terms) to convey their meaning. Possessing a large vocabulary is a sign of education. Knowing when to use the words in that vocabulary is a measure of wisdom. Word choice also can be a barrier when one uses general rather than specific words or phrases:

| General | Specific |
|---|---|
| vehicle (what type?) | minivan, sedan, SUV |
| book (what kind?) | dictionary, novel, mystery |
| several (how many?) | three, four, six |
| soon (when?) | by 11 a.m., before 3 p.m. |

Whenever possible, writers should use specific words and phrases and include whatever additional information the receiver needs to understand the message. In the preceding examples, the minivan could be described further by providing the year, make, model, and color. The dictionary could be described further by including its name, publisher, edition, and copyright date.

## Incorrect or Incomplete Content and Poor Organization

Messages must be accurate, complete, and well organized. Something as simple as using an incorrect day with a date confuses receivers and generates the need for additional communication. Further messages must also be exchanged when a message fails to provide all the information that a reader needs. Poor organization can obstruct communication. Telling a receiver to "immediately [do something]" and then saying "but not before you [do something else]" is confusing. Readers should not have to struggle to find or understand information.

*Do not use jargon unless you are sure your reader will understand it.*

*Choose specific, understandable words.*

*Messages must be:*
- *Accurate.*
- *Complete.*
- *Well organized.*

## Wrong Communication Channel

Sometimes a sender selects an inappropriate method by which to transmit a message (regular instead of express mail when a quick reply is needed, for example). When this happens, successful communication is jeopardized. Speed and the sender's relationship with the receiver are among the factors to consider when selecting a communication channel. This topic will be covered in greater detail in Chapter 2.

*Think carefully about the best method of transmitting your message.*

## Grammar, Spelling, and Punctuation Errors

Errors in grammar, spelling, and punctuation not only impede understanding but also reflect poorly on writers and the organizations they represent. Imagine the embarrassment of the attorney who pointed toward a chart with the heading "Calender of Job Search Activity" or the chagrin of the federal office worker who ordered pens bearing the words "Untied States." Proofreading is essential, even when electronic resources such as spell checkers are used.

*Use spelling and grammar tools before proofreading.*

## Receiver Mistakes

Although the sender has primary responsibility for removing communication barriers, the receiver also plays a role in good communication. The reader must give his or her full attention to the message and make a sincere effort to understand it. The receiver also has an obligation to provide feedback. **Verbal feedback** includes acknowledgements, questions, and comments; **nonverbal feedback** includes facial expressions and body language. Unless the receiver takes this role seriously, he or she actually creates a communication barrier.

*Be receptive; provide feedback.*

# WHY USE WRITTEN COMMUNICATION?

With all the potential obstacles to overcome, a sender might wonder why written communication is so common in the workplace. Written messages are popular for the following reasons:

1. Written messages are long-lasting. They can be filed for future reference. E-mails can be stored electronically or printed and stored in traditional files.
2. Written messages have legal value. Under certain conditions, letters and memos are treated as contracts.
3. Written messages can be revised many times before they are sent. The writer can check to be sure the content is correct. Sentences can be rearranged; words can be changed. Electronic resources such as spell checkers and grammar checkers can be used.

4. Written messages can be read as many times as needed be understood. This is very important if the message is complex.

5. Written messages can be directed to many receivers at different locations.

6. Written messages are convenient for both the sender and the receiver. The sender can prepare the message at a location other than an office and can do so during or outside regular work hours. The receiver may read the message at any time or any place.

[THINKING IT THROUGH 1-3]

## Selecting a Communication Medium

Although written messages have several advantages, they are not appropriate for every situation. Describe a situation in which you believe face-to-face or telephone communication would be better than written communication. Name your preferred method and explain why it would be more effective.

Situation:


Explanation:


# CHAPTER SUMMARY

- Effective communication is important to workers and the organizations that employ them.
- Communication may be described by its mode, destination, flow, and style.
- Messages should be ethical and legal.
- The written communication process involves a sender who encodes a message and transmits it to a receiver, who decodes it and gives feedback to the sender.
- Common barriers to communication are poor word choice; incorrect or incomplete content; poor organization; the wrong channel; grammar, spelling, and punctuation errors; and receiver mistakes.
- Written communications play an important role in the workplace because they can be kept, can serve as legal contracts, can be revised, can be read as many times as needed, can be sent to many recipients, and are convenient to write or read.

*Chapter 1: Understanding the Communication Process*

1. Consult the classified section of a local or regional newspaper that includes employment opportunities in your occupational field. How many of the advertisements list communication skills as a desired qualification? Are the references general (e.g., ability to communicate) or specific (e.g., write letters, greet clients)? Submit a list of your findings to your instructor.

2. Explain the meaning of each nonverbal signal in the following list.

   a.  a door being slammed _____

   b.  fingers tapping on a desk _____

   c.  laughter _____

   d.  clock watching during a meeting _____

   e.  a clenched fist _____

3. Indicate whether the following images illustrate an example of verbal communication (V), nonverbal communication (N), or both (B). Circle the appropriate response.

   a. V N B            b. V N B            c. V N B            d. V N B

4. What nonverbal messages are sent by the following letter?

   Dear Customer

   Thank you for letting us clean you furniture. So that we might continually strive to provide the sort of service you expect, we ask that you compleat the following questioneer.

   1. Was the clearner punctial?                                    Yes        No

   2. Was he or she neat?                                              Yes        No

   3. Was the carpet cleaned to your expections, considering age and ware?    Yes        No

   In appreciation for your timely response, here's a cupon for a free sandwich at Freddies on Fourth Street. The cupon can be used between November 20 and 31.
   A self-addressed envelop is inclosed.

   Nonverbal message: _____

   _____

   _____

5. Indicate whether the following items are internal or external messages (or could be either). Use *I* for *Internal* and *E* for *External*.

| Item | Internal or External |
|---|---|
| An annual report to stockholders | |
| A memo announcing that the third-floor cafeteria will be closed for six weeks during remodeling | |
| An e-mail telling customers about a spring sale | |
| An e-mail announcing that the company's founder died of a heart attack | |
| A get-well card from a manager to her administrative assistant | |
| A news release announcing plans to expand a corporation's U.S. headquarters | |
| A letter urging employees to complete a survey | |
| A Web page describing the company's health care program | |

6. **@ email** Assume that the retail store where you work as a cashier allows employees to buy merchandise for themselves and their immediate family at a 15 percent discount. One day, you overhear another cashier use the discount to buy a gift for her fiancé. Is the cashier's action illegal? Is it unethical? Present your opinions in an e-mail to your instructor. If e-mail isn't available, write your paragraph in the space provided below.

7. In the space provided at the top of the next page, rewrite or key this message, replacing the general words and phrases with specific ones.

We recently surveyed lots of our workers and learned that most would like some exercise equipment in the locker room. We checked around and found that we could buy a few pieces of equipment without spending lots of money. Of course, the locker room will need some remodeling. If you approve this proposal soon, we can have the work done fast.

8. The words in the following list were used in Chapter 1. Indicate whether each is in your use vocabulary, your recognition vocabulary, or neither. If you do not know the word, use a dictionary to check the meaning and write a brief definition in the space provided under "Neither."

| Word | Use Vocabulary | Recognition Vocabulary | Neither |
|---|---|---|---|
| chagrin | | | |
| contradictory | | | |
| demographic | | | |
| facilitate | | | |
| hamper | | | |
| impede | | | |
| integrity | | | |
| ironically | | | |
| jeopardized | | | |
| mode | | | |

9. What information is needed to make the following e-mail from a manager to her staff complete? Write your response in the space provided.

> Representatives of the local high school's business club will be selling merchandise to raise money for a trip to the group's national meeting. Please support this fundraiser.

10. Language can be a barrier to international communication, even when that language is English. Identify the North American English term for each British term in the following list. Use print or electronic resources to assist you.

a. car park _____

b. dustbin _____

c. flat _____

d. lift _____

e. loo _____

f. petrol _____

g. serviette _____

h. solicitor _____

i. torch _____

j. zebra crossing _____

11. Would you prefer to use oral or written communication in each of these situations? Why?

a. It's June 5. You just returned to work after a two-week vacation. When you check your voice mail, you find a message from Hayden Waldorff asking whether you will attend the computer training session scheduled for 9 a.m. June 6. You are planning to attend.

b. You're reading a long, detailed report. Suddenly, from the office next to yours, you hear loud voices and laughter. You wait five minutes, but the noise continues. You want the group to lower their voices.

c. Brenna Diaz, your supervisor, wants to know how much your department spent for cell phone service during the first quarter of the fiscal year. The records show the unit spent $2,044.69.

d. Paul Wrazidlo, your cousin who lives in another state, will graduate from Deluxe School of Design next week. You want to tell Paul how happy you are about his success.

# Planning Written Business Messages

"*Would you tell me, please, which way I ought to go from here?*"

"*That depends a good deal on where you want to get to,*" said the Cat.

"*I don't much care where—*" said Alice.

"*Then it doesn't matter which way you go,*" said the Cat.

At first glance, this quote from *Alice's Adventures in Wonderland* may not seem to have much to do with business writing. A closer look, however, reveals there is a strong, positive relationship between the quote and goal setting—an important element in planning business messages.

## PLAN BEFORE YOU WRITE

A **plan** is a set of steps or tasks that must be completed to reach a goal. Little in life gets done without planning, and communication is no exception. Sometimes planning occurs quickly—almost subconsciously, as for a quick e-mail to a friend. At other times, planning is slow and methodical, as for a formal report. The factors that affect the time and effort you spend on planning are (1) the complexity of the situation and (2) your familiarity with the task. The more complex or unfamiliar the task, the longer and more structured the planning must be.

During your first few weeks on a new job, you may be nervous. Your surroundings, your coworkers, and the tasks you perform may be unfamiliar to you and, therefore, may seem complex. At this stage, you will probably spend a great deal of time planning how to complete the tasks you are assigned. You may ask questions and take notes. If your work includes writing, you will probably prepare an outline and at least one draft before you finish a document.

As time passes, you will become more comfortable in your work environment and more confident about your ability to complete tasks efficiently and effectively. Planning will become more automatic and will take less time. When you write, you may not need to create an outline or many drafts. You will still *plan*, but the activity will be more mental than physical.

### LEARNING OBJECTIVES

- Recognize the role planning plays in the writing process.
- Identify the steps in planning a written business message.
- Implement the steps in the planning process.

*Planning is essential for good writing.*

### WORKPLACE CONNECTION

Much of the writing you do on the job is routine.

Planning saves time, reduces stress, minimizes communication barriers, and helps writers produce higher-quality messages. The process has five steps:

- **Step 1:** Determine your goals.
- **Step 2:** Analyze the situation and receiver.
- **Step 3:** Select the distribution method.
- **Step 4:** Identify content.
- **Step 5:** Gather materials and organize the message.

# STEP 1: DETERMINE YOUR GOALS

How do you measure personal success? You can use *quantitative* measures—GPA, salary, points scored, or pounds lost. You can use *qualitative* measures—contentment, happiness, or security. Whatever specific measure you choose, you determine success by comparing results to preset goals. The same is true in business communication.

Before beginning to write, it is important that you identify general and specific goals. All messages have both, and clarifying them is the first step in the planning process.

## General Goals

Determine the **general goal** by asking, "Why am I sending this message?" Frame your response broadly: to inquire, to inform, to persuade, or to build goodwill.

**INQUIRE.** To inquire is to ask a question. Your goal is to obtain data or information. The key to writing a successful inquiry is being specific. The following are examples of inquiry messages:

- A memo to the human resources department asking whether they have negotiated corporate discounts at any area health clubs.
- A letter to a supplier asking why a quantity discount was not applied to a bill.
- An e-mail to department members asking who has the software manual you need.

**INFORM.** Messages that inform provide information. A successful informative message has three characteristics: clarity, completeness, and timeliness. First, the message must be written clearly so the receiver will easily understand it. Second, the message must contain all the information the receiver needs to act or to decide. Third, the message must arrive in time for the receiver to consider it and act on its contents if necessary. The following are examples of messages that inform:

- A report detailing the costs and benefits of outsourcing janitorial services.

- A letter responding to a customer's request for information about delivery options.

- An e-mail canceling a planning committee meeting.

**PERSUADE.** Persuasive writing uses logic and/or emotion to influence a reader to react in a particular way. An effective persuasive message clearly states what to do and why. Persuasive messages stress how the reader will benefit from the proposed action. The following are examples of persuasive messages:

- A memo recommending the purchase of new furniture for a reception area.

- A flyer promoting an elementary school carnival.

- An e-mail encouraging employees to become organ donors.

**BUILD GOODWILL.** All messages should build goodwill between a sender and a receiver, but some messages have goodwill as their only goal. These messages are designed to make the reader feel important or special. They bring to the business environment the kindness and courtesy shown in personal or social interactions. The following are examples of goodwill messages:

- A handwritten note added to a sympathy card for your secretary, whose mother died last weekend.

- A letter congratulating a customer on receiving a prestigious community service award.

- A memo thanking a colleague for suggesting a more efficient way to process a claim.

Sometimes messages have more than one general goal. A message designed to convey bad news, for example, informs and persuades. The message *informs* readers of the negative information in a way designed to *persuade* them to accept the news or an alternative solution.

## Specific Goals

The **specific goal** of the message answers the questions "What results do I want?" and "What action do I want the receiver to take?" The following examples show the relationship between general and specific goals:

- **Message:**          A letter to clients of your insurance agency.
  **General Goal(s):**  To inform; to persuade.
  **Specific Goal:**    To announce a rate increase and retain policyholders.

- **Message:** An e-mail containing inventory data requested by your manager.
  **General Goal:** To inform.
  **Specific Goal:** To provide information to be used in planning future purchases.

- **Message:** A letter congratulating a client who recently received an award from the United Way.
  **General Goal:** To build goodwill.
  **Specific Goal:** To commend a client for her dedication and willingness to serve.

Recall from Chapter 1 that all messages, regardless of their general or specific goals, must be both legal and ethical.

[THINKING IT THROUGH 2-1]

## Determining the Goals of a Message

Identify the general and specific goals in the following messages:

1. A memo requesting $2,350 to attend a professional meeting in Hawaii.
   General Goal(s):_____
   Specific Goal:_____
   _____
   _____

2. A report describing the results of air quality tests done in an office area where several employees have experienced respiratory problems.
   General Goal(s):_____
   Specific Goal:_____

3. A letter to a government agency requesting clarification of a regulation.
   General Goal(s):_____
   Specific Goal:_____

4. A business expansion plan that will be submitted as part of a loan application.
   General Goal(s):_____
   Specific Goal:_____
   _____
   _____

5. A letter appealing the denial of a recently submitted health care claim.
   General Goal(s):_____
   Specific Goal:_____

# STEP 2: ANALYZE THE SITUATION AND RECEIVER

Both the situation and the receiver must be considered when you plan a writing strategy.

## The Situation

Assess the environment in which you and the receiver operate. Time, distance, equipment, the sensitivity of the situation, and your relationship with the receiver play a role in determining what, when, where, and how to communicate. Your analysis of the situation, together with your analysis of the receiver, will help you determine how to organize your message, the words you use, and the medium and channel through which you distribute the message.

## The Receiver

No two people are alike; no two people have the same experiences. These differences make people interesting and make writing a challenge.

Effective communicators choose words their receivers understand. They organize messages to hold a reader's attention. To do these things well, writers must learn all they can about the reader's *knowledge of the subject, interests and motivations*, and *demographic profile*. The writer must determine who will be the primary reader and focus on that person's needs.

> ## WORKPLACE
> ### CONNECTION
>
> The ability to interact positively with people from diverse backgrounds will make you an asset to your employer.

> *A single receiver may not behave the same way in two different situations.*

SEE THINGS FROM YOUR CUSTOMER'S POINT OF VIEW 50¢

GOFF

© 1996 Ted Goff

### SUBJECT KNOWLEDGE.

Assessing a receiver's knowledge of the subject about which you are communicating helps you determine content and choose words. A reader who is unfamiliar with a subject will not understand its jargon and will need a more detailed explanation than will a reader who is familiar with the subject. Similarly, a reader who already has some knowledge of a situation will need less background information than a reader who does not. Good writers make sure their readers are fully informed yet do not waste their time with unnecessary information.

### INTERESTS AND MOTIVATIONS.

Knowing what interests and motivates a receiver—in general *and* with respect to the situation about which you are communicating—helps you write from the receiver's viewpoint. Interests and motivations also influence the organization of the message and the words used. Identify subjects, words, ideas, and other factors to which the reader might be sensitive; avoid them or treat them with care.

Many theories of human motivation exist. One of the most notable theories was introduced by psychologist Abraham Maslow in 1943. Maslow believed that people are motivated by five levels of need. As basic needs near fulfillment, individuals move to other levels, seeking to satisfy those needs. Maslow's hierarchy of needs is shown in Figure 2-1.

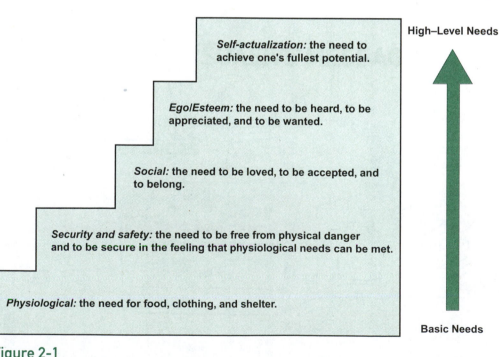

**Figure 2-1**
Maslow's Hierarchy of Needs

*Chapter 2: Planning Written Business Messages*

As you analyze your receiver, determine where the action you seek falls within Maslow's hierarchy. Also determine whether the individual with whom you are communicating will be more influenced by **extrinsic factors** (external, tangible; e.g., money or a promotion) or **intrinsic factors** (internal, emotional; e.g., pride in work or satisfaction).

DEMOGRAPHIC PROFILE.  A **demographic profile** is a factual picture of an individual or an organization. An individual's demographic profile includes age, race, gender, marital status, number of children, education, religion, occupation, and socioeconomic status. An organization's demographic profile includes size, location, number of employees, and products or services offered. Knowing the reader's demographic profile helps writers send an appropriate message.

Receiver and situation analysis are among the most complex activities associated with business communication. Your ability to analyze receivers will improve with experience. Be patient and persistent.

> *Demographics help you understand your reader.*

> *Recognize and respect individual differences.*

## [THINKING IT THROUGH 2-2]

## Receiver Analysis

Based on what you know about the following individuals, describe how you believe they would react to receiving notice that their tax return for last year has been selected for audit. How does each individual's educational background influence your opinion? What interests and motivations would each receiver have?

Yourself:

Your parents:

Your teacher:

Your best friend:

# STEP 3: SELECT THE DISTRIBUTION METHOD

Choosing a way to send your message is a two-part process. You must select the **medium** for the communication as well as the **channel** through which it will be distributed.

## The Medium

The **medium** is the form a message takes.

The four most common types of business messages are letters, memos, e-mail, and reports. Letters and memos are often referred to as correspondence. E-mail, though it serves a similar purpose, is typically not included in that classification. Each type of message, as well as instant messaging, is described briefly in the next sections.

Use letters for external messages or formal internal messages.

**LETTERS.** Businesses use letters to communicate with people outside the organization. For example, letters may be sent to shareholders, potential clients, current customers, suppliers, or government agencies. **Personal-business letters** are sent from individuals to organizations. Some organizations use letters to communicate with their employees about important personnel matters.

Letterhead stationery contains contact information for the sender's organization.

Letters are the most formal type of correspondence. They should be printed on good-quality bond paper imprinted with the company **letterhead**. A letterhead contains vital contact information for the organization. Name, address, and phone number have always been the "top three" in letterhead information. Including fax numbers, e-mail addresses, and Internet URLs is becoming commonplace.

A logo, a slogan, and the names of people who have key roles in the organization also may be displayed on its stationery. In large organizations, upper-level managers and individual departments have their own letterhead. Figure 2-2 shows examples of company and departmental letterhead stationery.

Organizations can create their own letterhead in word processing or other software and can print it in-house as needed. However, this is sometimes more costly and often more time-consuming than having letterhead stock prepared commercially. In addition, the results may be less attractive and professional.

Guidelines for preparing letters and memos are included in Appendix A.

A business letter should include the date, the complete name and mailing address of the receiver, a greeting, message content, a closing such as *Sincerely*, and a signature line. Wording should be conversational but not casual. Abbreviations and contractions should seldom be used. The formal appearance of a letter contributes to a positive image of the organization.

Use memos for internal messages.

**MEMOS.** When people within the same organization write to one another, they often use **memos**. The writer and reader may work at adjacent desks or in different countries—the location does not matter.

*Chapter 2: Planning Written Business Messages*

**M&C** Mason & Culver

214 S. High St.
Muncie, IN 47305-1621

PHONE: (765) 555-0116
Fax: (765) 555-0117
http://www.masonculver.com

**M&C** Mason & Culver

214 S. High St.
Muncie, IN 47305-1621

PHONE: (765) 555-0116
Fax: (765) 555-0117
http://www.masonculver.com

**Legal Dept.**
Room 400
(765) 555-0116

### Figure 2-2
Samples of Business Letterhead

You can create your own letterhead for personal use.

## WORKPLACE CONNECTION

Some companies have style manuals to describe the letter, memo, and report formats they want their employees to use.

A memo would be used, for example, to tell a worker that his or her vacation has been approved or to announce a contest that all employees are eligible to enter.

Memo formats are less formal than letter formats. A traditional memo includes "To," "From," "Date," and "Subject" headings, followed by the body of the memo. Word processing software **templates** offer the writer different design options. Because memos are internal documents, they often are prepared on a lower-quality bond letterhead or on plain paper.

Like the format, the writing style used for memos is typically less formal than that used for letters. More than one receiver's name may be listed in the heading. Courtesy and occupational titles usually are omitted. Abbreviations and contractions are used with greater frequency. Memos are courteous and respectful, but statements designed to build goodwill are not required. For example, a memo to notify participants about the agenda for a regularly scheduled meeting doesn't need a goodwill statement like "I'm looking forward to seeing you" at the end.

Memos are less formal than letters.

**E-MAIL.** Perhaps the most widely used distribution method today is **e-mail (electronic mail)**. The convenience, speed, and ease of e-mail prompt people to use it in place of telephone calls or face-to-face

E-mail is convenient, fast, and easy to use.

1. Include a brief, descriptive subject line that explains the theme of the message. Use leaders like URGENT or FYI when appropriate.

2. When replying to a message, include only as much of the original message as the reader needs to understand your response.

3. Keep messages readable by not exceeding one screen.

4. Send copies only to those who need them.

5. Never send e-mail when you are angry or upset.

6. Use asterisks (*good*) or italics—not capitals—for emphasis.

7. Use simple formatting. Avoid fancy fonts, symbols, colored text, and so on.

8. Fill in the address of the receiver after you write your message and are satisfied it is clear and complete.

9. Never say anything in e-mail you would not want made public. Messages can be forwarded and retrieved from system archives even after senders and receivers have deleted them. Courts have supported employers' right to read their employees' e-mails.

10. Learn about and use the features of your e-mail software. Most programs have a spell-check feature; some have a "retrieve" function to call back errant messages.

**Figure 2-3**
Tips for Sending E-Mail

meetings. As a result, messages sent via e-mail tend to be more conversational than those distributed in print.

Being conversational, however, does not mean discarding all basic writing rules and guidelines. Wise e-mail users analyze the receiver and the situation before crafting a message. Minor errors and shorthand may be acceptable in a message telling a workplace friend you're ready for lunch, but you will probably want to use complete sentences and spell words correctly when responding to an inquiry from your supervisor or a customer.

When preparing e-mails, apply the following guidelines, as well as the tips included in Figure 2-3.

- When using e-mail for internal communication, follow your company's writing style guidelines for memos.

- When using e-mail for external communication, follow the conventions for letters.

- When using e-mail for personal (nonbusiness) messages, use good judgment, courtesy, and respect.

Always follow your employer's guidelines for e-mail use.

**INSTANT MESSAGING.** Unlike e-mail, which can sit in the receiver's inbox unread, **instant messaging** (IM) occurs in real time, like a phone conversation or private chat room.

An increasing number of employees—in a recent survey, 27 percent—use instant messaging at work. These employees, often comfortable with IM from years of personal use, say instant messaging makes them more productive, yielding a quicker response than e-mail and helping them solve problems more rapidly. Employers, however, worry that IM poses security risks, can spread viruses, and is a distraction. Some of the concern stems from the potential for misunderstanding the many abbreviations used in instant messages. Figure 2-4 shows several of these abbreviations.

| 2DAY | today | ILBL8 | I'll be late |
|------|-------|-------|--------------|
| B/C | because | IMO | in my opinion |
| BTW | by the way | JK | just kidding |
| CID | consider it done | NC | no comment |
| F2F | face to face | OTOH | on the other hand |
| FYI | for your information | PCR | per customer request |

**Figure 2-4**
Sample IM Acronyms

**REPORTS.** **Reports** are documents that contain information, data analyses, or recommendations upon which decisions are based. Because of their versatility, reports are a special written communication medium. Their audience can be internal or external; their style, formal or informal. The more components—title page, table of contents, transmittal pages, sections, headings, footnotes, references, index, appendices—the report has, the more formal it is. Although formal reports tend to be longer than informal ones, length is *not* a measure of formality.

Informal reports may be less structured versions of formal reports (fewer components), or they may be formatted as letters or memos. Memo reports are for internal audiences; letter reports are for external audiences. Side headings can be included to guide the reader, just as the headings in this book help you understand the flow, organization, relationship among, and relative importance of items.

*Reports can be formal or informal.*

## The Channel

Your analysis of the situation and the receiver will help you determine the channel through which you transmit your message. **Channel** refers to the way a message is sent. Postal/courier services, fax, and e-mail are examples of channels. Choose a channel that is efficient and effective for the particular message you are sending. Factors to consider in choosing a channel include the following:

*Choose a message distribution channel that meets receiver needs.*

- Number of receivers
- Speed
- Cost
- Access (Does the recipient have and check e-mail, for example?)
- Privacy (E-mail, for example, is not suitable for sensitive messages.)
- Retention (Does the recipient need a written copy?)
- Receiver's preference

Appearance is another factor to consider. If it is important that a message look a certain way (in columns, for example), prepare it in word processing or spreadsheet software and either fax it or send it as an e-mail attachment. Either method ensures that the format will be retained during transmission, while standard e-mail does not.

The number of channels available for sending messages has expanded dramatically. Letters used to be delivered almost exclusively through the postal service, which offered several delivery classes and services. Courier service was also an option, but cost and distance made it impractical for widespread use.

Today, businesses use a number of delivery services that offer same-day or overnight options at competitive prices. For even faster service, electronic delivery is available by fax or via the Internet. Sometimes a message sender will use several channels. A letter can be sent electronically to take advantage of speed and in paper form for legal or other reasons.

Whether using a paper or an electronic channel, senders must be sure the receiver's mailing, fax, or e-mail address is correct. A simple character transposition can delay or prevent delivery.

## STEP 4: IDENTIFY CONTENT

The content of a message is determined by answering six critical questions: *Who? What? When? Where? Why?* and *How?* A writer should first answer these questions from his or her point of view. Then, he or she should assume the role of message receiver and answer the questions from that person's perspective. Only by looking at a situation from both sides can the writer be sure all essential information will be included in a message.

If the subject of the message is simple or routine, answer the six critical questions by jotting notes before you begin to write. When you respond to an e-mail, use the Reply function, and keep the message you are replying to on the screen until the response has been drafted. Then you can decide whether to delete the original message, edit it, or send it as is with your response.

For unfamiliar or complex writing tasks, writers often turn to **brainstorming** or **cluster diagramming**.

# Brainstorming

In **brainstorming**, writers list the items they *might* include in the message. Ideas are listed randomly, without regard to quality, form, order, or priority. One strength of brainstorming is that it can be done alone or with a group. Group brainstorming can be used even when only one person prepares and signs the message.

After the ideas have been recorded, review the list. Add, delete, or combine ideas to reflect the subject, receiver, situation, and goals of the message.

*During brainstorming, put down every idea you can think of. You can sort through and delete ideas later.*

# Cluster Diagramming

Cluster diagramming, like brainstorming, involves listing ideas without prejudging them. However, with **cluster diagramming**, related ideas are grouped as they are written. A writer might begin by listing the six critical questions. Answers are then written near the question to which they relate. As shown in Figure 2-5, main ideas can form the core of the diagram. Once the ideas have been listed, lines are drawn to connect related ideas. New ideas are added; duplicate ideas are deleted. Then, the ideas are evaluated for use in the final document.

*Like brainstorming, cluster diagramming involves listing as many ideas as possible.*

*Cluster diagrams help you see the relationships among ideas.*

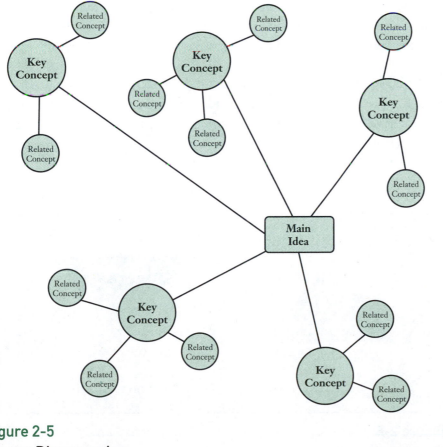

**Figure 2-5**
Cluster Diagramming

# STEP 5: GATHER MATERIALS AND ORGANIZE THE MESSAGE

After choosing the ideas to be included in a message, the writer gathers and organizes supporting materials.

## Gather Materials

The information to be included in a message can come from a variety of sources, including records kept by the organization. Depending on the data, the writer may need to access and review forms, correspondence, spreadsheets, databases, reports, manuals, or a variety of other in-house materials.

Pamphlets, brochures, books, journals, and the Internet may be useful external resources. Writers also may collect new data. Surveys, observations, and interviews are some ways to collect current data.

## Select an Organizational Approach

The final step in the planning process is organizing the message. The writer chooses a **direct** or an **indirect** pattern (see Figure 2-6).

**DIRECT ORGANIZATION.** Using a **direct** pattern means the writer presents the main idea first. Supporting facts or ideas are presented after the main idea. If the writer expects the reader to have a neutral or positive reaction to the message, the direct approach is best. This approach works well for messages designed to inquire, build goodwill, or inform.

**INDIRECT ORGANIZATION.** Writing **indirectly** means supporting ideas are presented before the main idea. This technique can be especially effective when writing to persuade or to convey bad news. If the writer expects the reader to have a negative reaction to the message, the indirect approach will have a greater chance of success.

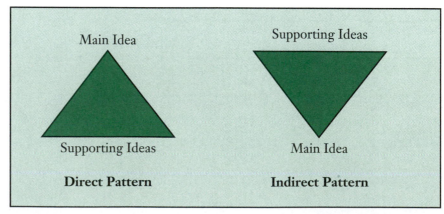

**Figure 2-6**
Organizational Plans

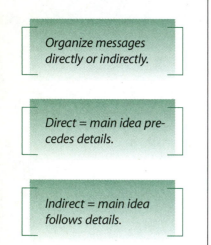

*Organize messages directly or indirectly.*

*Direct = main idea precedes details.*

*Indirect = main idea follows details.*

## Apply the Planning Process

As office manager for Metropolitan Clinic, you are often called upon to write letters and memos that will be reviewed and signed by the physicians. Today, you've been asked to prepare a message for Dr. Martin Martinez. One of his patients is moving to another state and has asked to have records forwarded to a physician there. After speaking briefly with Dr. Martinez, you identified the following ideas to include in the message:

A.  Good luck in new location.
B.  Records have been sent.
C.  Patient's son Jordan was first baby Dr. Martinez delivered.
D.  Appreciation
E.  Patient has a health-conscious family.

Answer the following questions based on your analysis of the situation and the receiver:

1.  What is your general goal?_____

2.  What is your specific goal?_____

3.  What medium will you choose?_____

4.  What channel will be best?_____

5.  What organizational approach will you use?_____

6.  How will you arrange the ideas to conform to that approach? (List by topic letter sequence; e.g., A, B, C.)

    _____

After 40 years as a general practitioner, Dr. Martinez will retire May 1. On behalf of the clinic where the doctor has practiced, you must notify patients of his impending retirement and encourage them to continue their care with a new physician who will join the clinic April 15.

7.  What is your general goal?_____

8.  What is your specific goal?_____

    _____

9.  What medium will you choose?_____

10. What channel will be best?_____

11. What organizational approach will you use?_____

▣ Time spent planning is time well spent. Good planning reduces the time spent in revising and helps ensure the success of the communication process.

▣ Follow these five planning steps for good writing:

1. **Determine your goals.** Always know why you are writing and what you expect to accomplish.

2. **Analyze the situation and receiver.** Learn all you can about the reader's knowledge of the subject, interests and motivations, and demographic profile.

3. **Select the distribution method.** Messages may take several forms and be distributed in numerous ways. Choices should be based on the receiver's needs while considering the sender's constraints.

4. **Identify content.** Ask yourself *Who? What? When? Where? Why?* and *How?* Use notes, brainstorming, or cluster diagramming to answer these questions and list the items to be included in a message.

5. **Gather materials and organize the message.** The information to be included in a message can come from a variety of sources. The two methods of organization are direct (main idea first) and indirect (supporting ideas first).

---

As workplaces become more culturally diverse, employees must learn to communicate effectively across cultures to avoid misunderstandings. When your audience includes people from a non-English speaking background (NESB), consider the following points:

■ NESB employees may have difficulty judging the tone of a message. For example, attempts at humor ("During the fire drill, exit quietly and try not to trample anyone on the way out") might be puzzling or offensive.

■ Idioms and slang (e.g., "I know you have a lot on your plate") can be especially hard for NESB people to understand.

■ Double negatives and question tags can confuse NESB employees. For example, the question "You won't forget the procedures, will you?" may be answered with yes for agreement rather than no for "No, I won't."

■ Expectations expressed as requests (e.g., "I'd like you to finish this by 5 p.m.") might be understood as optional.

Producing culturally sensitive business messages not only will help NESB employees feel more appreciated but will increase the likelihood that tasks will be completed the way you intended.

Adapted from *Everybody's Business: A Guide for Employers*, published by Workbase: The National Centre for Workplace Literacy & Language, Auckland, New Zealand, 1999.

1. Explain how the saying "People don't plan to fail. They fail to plan" relates to business communication.

2. Assume that you invited your boss to be the speaker at a meeting of a civic club to which you belong. Although you provided detailed information about the group, the occasion, and the location, your boss's presentation fell short of what you expected based on your assessment of his workplace presentations. Instead of being brief and lighthearted, the presentation was long and technical. In addition, the presentation left much to be desired: eye contact was poor, gestures were distracting, and delivery was monotone. You learned the next day that just before leaving the office, your boss was notified that a major customer had canceled an order. As program planner for the club, you must send your boss a thank-you note.

   Analyze the situation and the receiver. Consider subject knowledge, interests and motivations, demographics, and extrinsic or intrinsic factors.

   The situation:

   The receiver:

3.  Select one of the following topics—or one of your own, with the approval of your instructor. Use Internet or traditional library resources to locate a journal or magazine article that addresses the topic. Summarize the article in an e-mail to your instructor. Hand in a copy of the article, or provide the URL.

- Instant messaging as a business tool
- Gender communication in the workplace
- Intercultural communication
- Plagiarism

4. What interest or motivation might a 24-year-old single mother (2-year-old son) who works as a dental assistant have to read a message about each of the following topics? The message goals are shown in parentheses:

- Federal tax law changes (inform; persuade to use tax service)._____

  _____

- Two-day, out-of-state training program (inform; require to attend)._____

  _____

- Life insurance (persuade to buy term insurance)._____

  _____

- Stock market (persuade to invest in a mutual fund)._____

  _____

5. Write a paragraph describing a situation in which communication was strained or failed because the sender did not analyze the receiver. The situation can be one you observed or one in which you participated. The communication may have been oral or written.

6. For each of the following situations, indicate whether a business letter, a memo, a personal-business letter, or an e-mail would be most appropriate and whether the message should be organized directly or indirectly. For some situations, more than one message type may be appropriate.

| Situation | Message Type(s) | Approach |
|---|---|---|
| a. Cancel a travel club membership during the 30-day trial period. | | |
| b. Explain to a customer that equipment he or she left for service cannot be repaired. | | |
| c. Tell the workers in your office that the alarm system will be tested at 2 p.m. on Wednesday. | | |
| d. Encourage your supervisor to cancel the weekly staff meeting scheduled for 3 p.m. on December 31. | | |
| e. Terminate the cleaning service your company has used for many years because of poor performance this year. | | |
| f. Notify employees that the lights are on in a car parked in the lot next to the building. | | |

7. The senior center where you volunteer has asked for your help in designing a letterhead. Here is their contact information:

The Havens, 50 Hatfield Road, Hamilton, MA 01982-1821
Phone: 978/555-0174  Fax: 978/555-0176
Website: http://www.havensofhamilton.com

Use word processing or other software to design an appropriate letterhead.

8. Through what channel would you distribute the message appropriate for each of the following situations? Justify your choice.

It's Saturday afternoon and you have a question about the accounting assignment that's due Monday. Your instructor encourages students to contact her when they have questions.

A member of your staff received a community service award, and you want the other members of your department to know of the recognition.

A manager in your field office (located in another state) urgently needs a copy of the audit letter you received yesterday.

You work in a large office building with a reception desk in the lobby. This morning, you overheard the receptionist soothe an angry visitor. You want to tell her and her supervisor how impressed you were by the way she handled the situation.

9.  Your supervisor has asked you to investigate the purchase of software to enable workers at remote locations to brainstorm about a collaborative report they are to prepare. Do an Internet search to locate appropriate software. Report your findings in a table with the following headings:

**Software Name      Cost      Core Features      URL for Site**

If you do not have Internet access, draw on your personal experiences with group work and prepare a table that lists at least five features you would seek in collaborative writing software and explains why each feature would be valuable. Use "Software Feature" and "Rationale" as headings in your table.

10. Divide your class into two groups. Each group is to decide what content to include in a document titled "E-mail Use Policy at [name of your school]." One group will use brainstorming, and the other will create a cluster diagram.

11. Collect samples of three business messages. Read each message to determine the general and specific goal and whether it uses the direct or indirect approach. Summarize your findings in an informal report to your instructor.

# Developing Business Messages

Once the planning process has been completed, you'll be ready to put your thoughts into words and to draft your business message. You'll polish that draft and, after proofreading, have a document ready to be sent to your receiver. By applying several principles as you draft, revise, edit, and proofread, you'll ensure your communication is accurate, professional, and likely to succeed.

## APPLYING THE 4Cs OF GOOD BUSINESS WRITING

The primary goal of all communication is receiver understanding. Business writing has the additional goals of being efficient and promoting goodwill. To meet these goals, writers apply principles of good writing known as "the 4Cs"—clarity, completeness, conciseness, and correctness.

### Clarity

**Clarity** is achieved when the receiver understands a message as the sender intended. Word choice, unity, coherence, and structure affect clarity. Each of these factors is described more fully in the following paragraphs.

**WORD CHOICE.** Choose short, familiar words your receiver will understand. Use *try* rather than *endeavor*, *guess* rather than *supposition*, and *warning* rather than *admonition*. A print or electronic thesaurus is a valuable tool in choosing clear, simple words.

Clear words are often called "talk" words because they are used in day-to-day speaking. Slang is also part of day-to-day speaking, but it is too casual to be used in business writing. Because slang varies by age, gender, culture, and region, its meaning may not be clear to a larger audience.

**Jargon** is occupational terminology. The words may be new terms or common ones used in uncommon ways. *Noise*, *bus*, *culture*, and *virus* have different meanings depending on the profession of those who use them; *debit* and *credit* are part of the jargon of accounting.

## LEARNING OBJECTIVES

- Apply the 4Cs of good business writing—clarity, completeness, conciseness, and correctness.
- Use a positive, unbiased, reader-centered tone.
- Draft business messages.
- Overcome writer's block.
- Revise, edit, and proofread business messages.

*Choose words that are short and familiar to the receiver.*

## WORKPLACE CONNECTION

When communicating across cultures, use English that is jargon-free and that avoids idioms, buzzwords, clichés, humor, and slang.

## "To access soup, interface opener tool and rotate can to reformat container configuration."

Use jargon only when you are certain your receiver will understand it. If you find it necessary to use jargon but are not sure your receiver will understand it, explain each word simply the first time you use it. After the word has been defined, you can use it freely.

Be cautious, too, when using abbreviations and acronyms. An **abbreviation** is a shortened version of a word. *Co.* (Company), *Dept.* (Department), and *Mgr.* (Manager) are abbreviations. An **acronym** is a word formed from the initial letters of major parts of a compound term. *FTE* (full-time equivalent) and *CPU* (central processing unit) are acronyms. Some acronyms are pronounced as words, such as *ESOP* (employee stock ownership plan) and *LIFO* (last in, first out). Abbreviations and acronyms that are meaningful to you may be meaningless and confusing to your receiver.

Another type of wording to avoid is the cliché. A **cliché** is a word or phrase that has been so overused it has become trite. Look for fresh alternatives to classic clichés such as *strike while the iron is hot* and *up a creek without a paddle* as well as more contemporary clichés such as *thinking outside the box*.

Concrete words are more understandable than abstract words. **Concrete** words convey one—and only one—meaning. They are specific and vivid. **Abstract** words are vague and imprecise. They may mean different things to different people. *Many* is less specific than *most*. *Most* could be made more specific by stating a number or percent. *Vehicle*

---

**Use jargon and abbreviations carefully.**

❝ *There is enormous power in stating something simply and well.* ❞

**-Pat Conroy**

**Choose specific words.**

is less specific than *car* or *truck*. *Car* and *truck* could be made more specific by adding details such as make, model, style, age, and color. Be as specific as necessary to convey the desired meaning to your receiver.

## [THINKING IT THROUGH 3-1]

## Choosing Simple, Concrete Words

1. Assume you are writing to someone with an eighth-grade education. Use a print or electronic thesaurus to find three words that can be used in place of each of the following words.

   a. capitulate _____

   b. expeditious _____

   c. impeccable _____

   d. juxtaposition _____

   e. pragmatic _____

2. Write a concrete word or expression for each of the following abstract words.

   a. fast _____

   b. later _____

   c. small _____

   d. soon _____

   e. whenever _____

UNITY.    Sentences and paragraphs have **unity** when they have one main idea and the other information in the sentence supports that main idea. The first sentence in each of the following sets lacks unity. Unity is improved in the second sentence of each set.

> Today is Monday; we are going to London soon.
> Today is Monday; on Thursday we leave for London.

> The report must be edited; the photocopier needs repair.
> By the time we finish editing the report, the photocopier should be fixed.

The most common way to create unity within a paragraph is to include a topic sentence. A **topic sentence** tells what a paragraph is about. It expresses the paragraph's main idea. A topic sentence may be the first or last sentence in the paragraph. In direct construction, the topic sentence opens the paragraph; in indirect construction, it ends the paragraph. The approach used within a message may vary from paragraph to paragraph. You may recognize these patterns as being similar to the approaches used to organize messages.

*Each sentence and paragraph should have one main idea.*

*Remember that paragraphs are organized by either the direct or the indirect approach.*

Messages should flow smoothly from idea to idea.

Transitional words and phrases link ideas.

**COHERENCE.** Unified messages are also **coherent**. They flow naturally, and the ideas in them relate to each other. Transitional words and phrases and repetition help make messages coherent.

*Transitional words and phrases.* Writers use transitional words and phrases as bridges to join ideas. Transitional words and phrases introduce additional information, show cause and effect, highlight comparisons and contrasts, and point out sequence and time. Each of these common transition types is illustrated in the following examples:

| Type of Transition | Transitional Word or Phrase |
|---|---|
| additional information | also, in addition, moreover, too, again |
| cause and effect | because, for this reason, therefore, thus, unless, consequently, as a result |
| comparison | likewise, similarly, in comparison, as |
| contrast | although, even though, but, however, in contrast, nevertheless, on the contrary, still, yet, on the other hand |
| sequence | first, second, etc.; next, then, last, finally; 1, 2, 3; a, b, c |
| time | before, after, then, at the same time, at that time, during, in the meantime, currently, previously, soon, while, now |

**Figure 3-1**
Transitional Words and Phrases

Repetition connects ideas and can make text read more smoothly.

*Repetition.* Repeating words and using pronouns in place of nouns are other ways to achieve coherence. The following sentences show these methods:

The pen and pencil **sets** are packed 12 to a box. Each **set** comes in a case that has the look and feel of leather. (repetition)

The pen and pencil **sets** are packed 12 to a box. **They** are available in gold, silver, or wood-grain casings. (pronouns)

### Office Jargon for the 21st Century

**blamestorming:** sitting around in a group discussing why a deadline was missed or a project failed and who was responsible

**cube farm:** an office filled with cubicles

**ego surfing:** searching the Internet for references to oneself

**mouse potato:** the online generation's answer to the couch potato

**prairie dogging:** when something loud happens in a cube farm and people's heads pop up over the walls to see what's going on

**uninstalled:** euphemism for being fired

**SwiftTech Software**

## Writing With Unity

Write a one- or two-paragraph description of your career goals. Use at least two of the transitions described in the preceding section.

---

**STRUCTURE.** Sentence structure can make a message more interesting and enhance clarity. To create interest, use a mixture of simple, compound, complex, and compound-complex sentences. To enhance clarity, eliminate dangling and misplaced modifiers and lack of parallelism.

*Varying the structure of sentences creates interest.*

    *Sentence structure.* English has four sentence structures. An example of each follows:

| | |
|---|---|
| *Simple*: | One main clause (subject and verb). Sue will take the package to Ron. |
| *Compound*: | Two main clauses. |
| | Sue will take the package to Ron; Sue will take the package to Ron; he is waiting for it. |
| *Complex*: | One main clause and one or more subordinate (dependent) clauses. |
| | Before she sorts the mail, Sue will take the package to Ron. |
| *Compound-Complex*: | Two main clauses and at least one subordinate (dependent) clause. |
| | Before she sorts the mail, Sue will take the package to Ron; he is waiting for it. |

*Dangling modifiers.* A modifier "dangles" when it modifies the wrong subject or when the true subject is not stated clearly in the sentence. Here are two examples:

While flying to Phoenix, my glasses broke.
To get a good job, computer skills are essential.

These sentences are unclear because the subjects cannot logically perform the actions described in the modifiers. Glasses cannot fly a plane; computer skills do not apply for jobs. Eliminate a dangling modifier by giving it a subject or changing the main clause so the subject applies to the modifier.

During **my** flight to Phoenix, my glasses broke.
To get a good job, **business graduates** must have computer skills.

Will you hire me?

**Figure 3-2**
Dangling Modifiers Make Meaning Unclear

*Place modifiers near the words to which they refer.*

*Misplaced modifiers.* A sentence may be unclear when a modifier is too far from the word(s) to which it relates. Notice how the meaning of each of the following sentences changes depending on where the modifier is placed:

**Only** I have keys to the only building. (one person has keys)
I **only** have keys to the building. (keys to nothing else)
I have the **only** keys to the building. (one set of keys)
I have keys to the **only** building. (one building)

Please let me know the status of the account on **July 31**. (refers to account status on a particular date)
On **July 31**, please let me know the status of the account. (specifies when status is to be reported)

*Use parallel structure.*

*Parallelism.* Elements in a series or list or joined by a conjunction should be treated in the same manner—nouns matched with nouns, verbs with verbs, and so on. The following sentences illustrate this concept:

| *Not Parallel:* | Please respond by phone or sending an e-mail. |
| *Parallel:* | Please respond by phone or e-mail. |

| *Not Parallel:* | The speech was lively, interesting, and motivated us. |
| *Parallel:* | The speech was lively, interesting, and motivational. |

| *Not Parallel:* | The candidate is not only interested in protecting the environment but also in creating jobs. |
| *Parallel:* | The candidate is interested not only in protecting the environment but also in creating jobs. |

## [THINKING IT THROUGH 3-3]

# Correcting Faulty Structure

Rewrite the following sentences to correct any structural problems they may contain. If the sentence has no errors, write *correct*.

1. While waiting for the bus, a limousine stopped in front of the hotel.

2. Before locking the door, the alarm was set.

3. As I approached the conference room, I heard laughter and people clapping.

4. The television station is limited in the amount of programming it can offer by hardware and finances.

5. My hobbies are jogging, reading, and working crossword puzzles.

6. Dylan was impressed and appreciative of Rosalee's remarks.

## Completeness

A message is complete when all the information necessary for a receiver to understand and act is included. What information is necessary depends on the writing situation. If questions have been asked, answer them. If a particular action is desired, specify it. If names, dates, locations, or figures are required for the receiver to take action, include them. Be sure you have asked and answered the questions *Who? What? When? Where? Why?* and *How?*

## [ THINKING IT THROUGH 3-4 ]

## Writing Complete Messages

You received the following e-mail, which was sent through a mailing list that reaches all employees in your organization:

> If you need a desk, table, or file cabinet for your office, let me know. We have extras.

> James Grotto
> Records Dept.
> Ext. 8021

1.  What information do you need to take advantage of this offer?

2.  What options do you have for getting the information you need?

3.  Which option will get you the information most quickly? Why?

*Chapter 3: Developing Business Messages*

# Conciseness

Busy business professionals prefer messages that express thoughts in the fewest words possible. Well-written business messages are only long enough to present all the necessary information.

Balance conciseness and clarity.

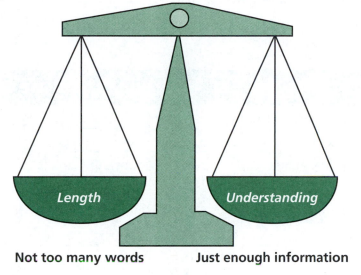

Length        Understanding

**Not too many words        Just enough information**

**Figure 3-3**
Balance Conciseness and Clarity

The key to writing concise messages, ones that are brief yet effective, is to make every word count. Limit repetition, eliminate excess words, emphasize verbs, and use the active voice.

**LIMIT REPETITION.**   Repeating a word or an idea is one way to emphasize it. Too much repetition, however, makes for dull and wordy writing. Two hints for reducing repetition are:

> *The most valuable of all talents is that of never using two words when one will do.*
> **-Thomas Jefferson**

*Reduce repetition.*

1. Use a shortened form of a noun.
2. Use a pronoun in place of a noun.

*Original:*    Johan Erickson was office manager for Ador and Smith from June 11, 2000, until February 27, 2005. Johan Erickson was efficient and effective. Johan Erickson worked well with the employees he supervised and scheduled the work of the employees he supervised to ensure prompt, correct completion of tasks assigned to the employees.

*Revision:*    Johan Erickson was office manager for Ador and Smith from June 11, 2000, until February 27, 2005. **Johan** was efficient and effective. **He** worked well with the employees he supervised and scheduled **their** work to ensure prompt, correct completion of **their** assigned tasks.

## ELIMINATE EXCESS WORDS.
A word is excess if it is not needed for correct grammar or clear meaning. Shorten sentences beginning with *It is*, *There is*, or *There are*. Minimize use of *that*. Delete *up*, *down*, *over*, and *under* unless they show position or location. Use adjectives and adverbs sparingly. Eliminate overused expressions such as *bottom line*, *win-win situation*, and *user-friendly*. Rather than use two words with the same meaning, delete one. Whenever possible, use a phrase instead of a clause, a word instead of a phrase.

| Wordy | Concise |
|---|---|
| There are three people who can | Three people can |
| at the time that we were meeting | while we met |
| move up to Canada | move to Canada |
| combine together | combine |
| in the vicinity of | near |
| send back | return |
| at the present time | now |
| due to the fact that | because |
| the meeting on May 10 | the May 10 meeting |

Vary sentence and paragraph length to hold the reader's interest. A good length for sentences in letters and memos is between 15 and 20 words. Paragraphs of four to six *lines* look inviting and encourage the receiver to keep reading.

Sentences and paragraphs in reports may be longer than those in letters and memos. Because reports are often formal and may contain technical information, sentences in them can range from 20 to 25 words, and paragraphs often contain eight to ten lines.

## EMPHASIZE VERBS.
Verbs are the most powerful words in the English language. Stressing verbs makes writing concise, clear, and powerful.

| Weak | Powerful |
|---|---|
| find a solution | solve |
| conduct an investigation | investigate |
| make a contribution | contribute |
| be a participant | participate |
| completed the reorganization | reorganized |
| made a selection | selected |

## USE THE ACTIVE VOICE.
The active voice tells *who* is doing *what*; it stresses the doer of the action. The passive voice tells *what* was done by

*Chapter 3: Developing Business Messages*

or to *whom* or *what*. It stresses the receiver of the verb's action and typically includes one of these words: *be, am, is, are, was, were,* or *been.* By using the active voice, writers create sentences—and messages—that are concise, direct, and forceful.

*Active Voice:*   John will conduct a cost-benefit analysis.
*Passive Voice:*   A cost-benefit analysis will be conducted by John.

*Active Voice:*   The members elected Carlos Esteban.
*Passive Voice:*   Carlos Esteban was elected by the members.

*Active Voice:*   You have not paid your April bill.
*Passive Voice:*   Your April bill has not been paid.

In the third example, the active voice sentence is a bit *too* forceful; it accuses the reader of not paying a bill. When using the active voice produces a negative effect, use the passive voice instead. In the example, using the passive voice places emphasis on the bill, not the reader.

Caution: Do not confuse voice with tense. The active voice may be used with present, past, and future tense verbs.

*The passive voice is more tactful.*

## [THINKING IT THROUGH 3-5]

## Writing Concise Messages

Rewrite the following paragraph to make it more concise by limiting repetition, eliminating excess words, using strong verbs, and writing in the active voice.

Reference manuals are certainly valuable tools and definitely wonderful resources for business professionals who write or prepare business messages as part of the work they do. A reference manual may be thought of by writers as a style guide or a "how to" book for writing. Typically, there is information in most of these reference manuals about grammar, punctuation, capitalization, abbreviations, word division, use of numbers and symbols, and proofreading. Some of these reference manuals also have special additional sections devoted to topics such as technology, filing, and getting a job.

## Correctness

Errors can be costly.

A message is correct when content and mechanics are accurate. Check facts (dates, figures, names), grammar, spelling, and punctuation. Errors can be costly. A misplaced decimal or an incorrect digit in a price or an account balance could cause a company to lose money. Grammar and punctuation errors can affect meaning and create a poor impression of writers and their organizations. Misspelling a name could annoy the receiver and result in a serious loss of goodwill and business. Consider the following examples:

- A manager received an invitation to speak at a luncheon. The date of the event was given as Monday, May 5. A glance at the calendar told the manager that May 5 was a Tuesday. Which was correct, the day or the date? Further communication was needed to clarify the request. The message was inefficient, ineffective, and possibly irritating.

- An organization printed catalogs and order forms and distributed them to 10,000 people. Customers were offered a 25 percent discount on orders of $500 or more. The company intended to offer a 2.5 percent discount. More than 800 orders were received before the error was discovered. The company had to choose between losing thousands of dollars or losing goodwill and customers. A corrected order form and letter of explanation were printed and mailed. Requests for the 25 percent discount were honored.

- Pat Petersen wrote to her insurance agent asking about special coverage for her computer. She received a prompt response—addressed to Mr. Pat Pedersen. Goodwill was damaged. The message was less than effective. Pat wondered whether she could trust information provided by an agent who doesn't recognize the importance of knowing each client's gender and name.

Check accuracy twice.

The accuracy of a message should be checked twice. Content should be checked during revision; mechanics should be checked during editing. Always proofread a document before it is signed or sent.

# WRITING IN A POSITIVE, UNBIASED, READER-FOCUSED TONE

Readers react best to messages written with a positive, unbiased, reader-focused tone.

## Positive Tone

Readers respond best to a positive tone.

To write with a positive tone, limit the number of negative words in a message. Avoid *no*, *not*, and *never*. Minimize the use of words with negative prefixes such as *dis-*, *im-*, *in-*, and *un-*. Consider each word you use and the impact it will have on your receiver. The words in the following list are among those to which people may react negatively.

| | | |
|---|---|---|
| allege | fault | irritate |
| bad | flaw | limit |
| claim | hate | loss |
| contrary | ignorant | nonsense |
| disagree | immature | penalty |
| disappoint | inadequate | ridiculous |
| error | inconsiderate | stupid |
| fail | inept | unable |

Writers also should use a positive tone. Rather than saying what cannot be done, say what can be done. Rather than saying what is wrong, say what is right. Focus on solutions, not problems. Here are examples:

*Negative Tone:* The door on Michigan Street will be locked.
*Positive Tone:* The door on First Avenue will be open.

*Negative Tone:* Model 113 has not been made since 2002.
*Positive Tone:* Model 113 has been replaced by Model 114.

*Negative Tone:* The sweater is not available in brown.
*Positive Tone:* The sweater is available in red, blue, and black.

## Unbiased Tone

Business writers should address all people with respect and recognize them for their abilities and talents. Good business messages do not stereotype people based on their gender or physical condition.

GENDER. Because both men and women contribute to the success of a business, writers should eliminate sexist language from their messages. Here are some ways in which this can be done:

> *Use gender-neutral language.*

1. Make the noun and pronoun plural.

   *Biased:* A **manager** should be interested in the professional development of **his** workers.
   *Neutral:* **Managers** should be interested in the professional development of **their** workers.

   Be careful to make both the noun and the pronoun plural. Pluralizing one but not the other creates a grammar error (pronoun/antecedent disagreement).

2. Delete the pronoun.

   *Biased:* Each candidate presented **his** ideas for cutting taxes.
   *Neutral:* Each candidate presented ideas for cutting taxes.

**WORKPLACE CONNECTION**

Recognize your personal biases and set them aside when you communicate.

**3.** Use an article (*a*, *an*, *the*) in place of the pronoun.

*Biased*: Every cashier should keep **her** counter free of clutter.
*Neutral*: Every cashier should keep the counter free of clutter.

**4.** Use both masculine and feminine pronouns.

*Biased*: A programmer should document the code **he** writes.
*Neutral*: A programmer should document the code **he or she** writes.
*Neutral*: A programmer should document the code **s/he** writes.

If the result sounds awkward, choose another method.

**5.** Choose job titles that do not indicate gender.

| Biased | Neutral |
|---|---|
| chairman | chair, head, leader |
| mailman | mail carrier |
| repairman/serviceman | service representative, technician |
| salesman | sales representative, agent |

**[THINKING IT THROUGH 3-6]**

# Writing Without Gender Bias

Rewrite the following sentences to eliminate gender bias.

1. A user can access his personal account at any time.

   _____

2. Every nurse should submit her continuing education certificates to her supervisor.

   _____

3. Someone left his cell phone in the computer lab.

   _____

4. Most businessmen would probably favor the plan.

   _____

5. A mechanic should keep his tools in good condition.

   _____

6. Anyone can find his way around the campus.

   _____

Most biased language stereotypes women, but men also can be affected by sexism. The terms *male nurse* and *male teacher* are just as biased as the terms *female doctor* and *female executive*. Wording that implies a person is unusual because he or she is in a particular profession should be changed.

Do not apply gender terms to groups of workers. Phrases such as *the girls in the office*, *the boys in the print shop*, and *the guys at work* should be changed. *The staff in the office*, *the workers in the print shop*, and *the people at work* are not only clear but also fair.

Unbiased language is fair language.

**PHYSICAL CONDITION.** A person's physical condition should be viewed apart from his or her ability to do a job. A person whose vision is other than 20/20 has a vision problem. A person with one leg has a mobility problem. These physical conditions become handicaps only when they limit a person's ability to complete a task or perform an action. Glasses or contact lenses improve a person's vision; an artificial limb, crutches, a cane, or a wheelchair improves a person's mobility.

Stress a person's ability.

When writing about someone who has a disability, decide whether it is necessary to mention the person's physical condition. Does describing Roberto Sequira as a *deaf accountant* add meaning to a message? Probably not. If the main idea of the message is the reader's need to use sign language or special communication equipment, say so. When it is necessary to refer to a disability, give the person ownership of the condition. A person who has a cold is not referred to as cold; a person who has a developmental disability should not be referred to as mentally retarded. Here's another example:

*Poor*: A ramp will be installed at the west entry for **people who are confined to wheelchairs**.

*Good*: A ramp will be installed at the west entry to provide access for **people who use wheelchairs**.

## Reader-Focused Tone

As you write, imagine yourself seated in your reader's home or office. Picture yourself opening the message and reading it. Does the message reflect the writer's interest in you or your business? Is the message warm and sincere? If the message focuses on the receiver and stresses how she or he will benefit, it is written from the reader's viewpoint.

Write from the receiver's point of view.

*Writer Focus*: I was impressed by the sales presentation you made.

*Reader Focus*: Your sales presentation was impressive!

*Writer Focus*: I am glad that you have accepted my invitation to the meeting.

*Reader Focus*: Thank you for agreeing to attend the meeting.

| | |
|---|---|
| *Writer Benefit*: | If I receive your vacation request by May 3, I can complete the schedule on time. |
| *Reader Benefit*: | If vacation requests are submitted by May 3, the schedule can be posted by May 15. |

Using the personal pronouns *you* and *your* won't guarantee that a message will stress the reader's point of view. In some cases, changing from the active to the passive voice is a good choice.

| | |
|---|---|
| *Writer Focus*: | I did not understand the e-mail you sent. |
| *Reader Focus but* | |
| *Negative Tone*: | You sent an e-mail that was confusing. |
| *Neutral Tone*: | Will you clarify the e-mail you sent? |

## DRAFTING BUSINESS MESSAGES

The work you did during the planning stage of the writing process will help you draft your message. The outline or list of ideas you created and the organizational plan you selected will be your guide as you convert your thoughts to words, sentences, and paragraphs.

Your goal during this stage of the writing process is to get something on paper. Focus on content and logic. Don't worry about grammar, spelling, punctuation, format, or other mechanical factors. Worrying about the mechanical aspects of a draft adds unnecessary pressure and detracts from the primary objective. Once your thoughts have been converted to words, the message can be shaped and refined through revision and editing.

Despite thorough planning, some people have difficulty starting to write. Rather than face a blank sheet of paper or a blank computer screen, some writers stall. They look for other things to do. They wait for inspiration. They want the words to flow in final form. They have **writer's block**.

Luckily, writer's block is temporary and usually can be overcome easily. The following techniques can subdue writer's block:

- **Commit to the task.** If writing is an important part of your job, establish a routine. Find a time when you have no commitments and when you know you will be effective. If you are most productive in the morning, make writing one of the first things you do after you arrive at work. Make writing part of your daily routine; let others know you are not to be disturbed during this activity.

- **Clear your mind.** If your head is full of nagging problems or you feel tense or nervous, you won't perform at your peak. Solve problems or set them aside. Take a five- or ten-minute break, perhaps a short walk; a change of scenery can help to clear your head and relieve stress.

*A draft is a work in progress.*

*Writer's block can be overcome.*

- **Get organized.** Be sure your work area is clean, comfortable, and functional. You will need easy access to files, research notes, a thesaurus, a dictionary, and a reference manual.

- **Plan first.** Even hastily written notes or a mental outline can help focus your thoughts.

- **Set short-term goals.** You can't finish something you haven't started. Set achievable goals and follow through. Your goal can be as simple as writing for five minutes without stopping (free write) or generating two paragraphs before lunch or a scheduled appointment.

- **Be patient.** If you have trouble with the opening of a message, write another section first. The opening will be easier when you return to it.

- **Remember, it's a *draft*.** The beauty of the writing process is that you can review and change what you've written before it is sent.

Once your message has been developed, let some time pass before you look at it again. The time needn't be long—just enough to give you a fresh perspective. If you are writing an e-mail, you might set it aside long enough to read one or two new messages. When you resume writing, you'll have a different perspective and can see where changes are needed.

## REVISING, EDITING, AND PROOFREADING BUSINESS MESSAGES

Revising and editing are separate processes with separate goals. **Revising** focuses on content; **editing** addresses mechanics. Some writers like to revise and edit on the computer. Others prefer to print the document and make notations on the paper copy, making changes on the computer later. The symbols presented in Appendix B are used to indicate changes when revising, editing, and proofreading printed copy.

### Revising

When writers revise messages, they verify content, delete or add material, move text to achieve better flow, strengthen word choice, smooth transitions, and improve tone. They also set the format. Revising may be done alone or with someone else. Reading a message aloud can help, too.

Familiarize yourself with features of your word processing software that will help you in revising. Three useful features for refining text are cut, paste, and thesaurus. Word processing software has many features that make formatting easy. They include fonts and type sizes, text alignment and other paragraph formatting options, automatic bullets and numbering, and headers and footers.

> *Let time pass between drafting and revising a message.*

> *Revising and editing are related, yet different.*

## WORKPLACE CONNECTION

Occasionally asking for help is a sign of strength, not weakness. It demonstrates a commitment to the organization and to the receiver.

**GET A SECOND OPINION.** When messages are long, have complex content, or deal with sensitive topics, it is wise to consult one or more colleagues as you revise. Explain the situation, and ask your coworker to read your draft. Get specific suggestions about how to strengthen content and style.

**READ ALOUD.** Reading your message aloud adds another dimension to the revising process. Hearing your message will heighten your awareness of gaps or weaknesses in logic or rough transitions between topics or ideas. You'll also get a better sense of whether you've used conversational language and have achieved an appropriate, businesslike tone.

## Editing

Business writers revise messages to refine content; they edit and proofread to be sure their messages are mechanically accurate.

During editing, writers check that spelling, grammar, punctuation, and format are correct. They pay special attention to items that spell checkers will miss such as names and frequently confused words. They make sure that grammar is correct, especially in areas that often pose problems: subject-verb agreement, pronoun-antecedent agreement, modifier placement, possessive formation, and parallelism. They ensure that the punctuation they have used is correct and consider opportunities to use additional punctuation to their advantage (for example, using a semicolon to join two independent clauses to show a strong relationship between ideas). They also check to be sure all required elements are included (e.g., enclosures, copy notations and that placement, headings, and other features enhance readability ideas).

Editing is an important process. Spelling and grammar errors can inhibit understanding, have an adverse effect on image, or both. Mechanics and format complement content and deserve serious attention.

## Proofreading

Proofreading is the final step in producing a document, the last check of your finished work. It involves reading the document closely, either alone or with a partner. Proofreading requires concentration. Because writers have created and revised message content, they tend to see what they think the message says, not what is really there. Fortunately, a number of methods, tips, and tools provide assistance.

Research suggests that printing a document before proofreading reduces the number of overlooked errors. When proofreading a printed page, try tilting the paper but not your head; the uncommon angle will force you to concentrate. When printing is not an option or when the message is brief, scroll through the text line by line. The

---

*Some errors can be heard more easily than seen.*

## WORKPLACE CONNECTION

Reading text aloud while editing can help you locate excess words, passive constructions, and boring or confusing sections.

## WORKPLACE CONNECTION

Make a list of the writing errors you make most often. Post the list near your computer as a reminder to watch for and correct those errors.

bottom border of the monitor will act as a visual barrier, forcing you to concentrate on one line at a time. The tips in Figure 3-4 will help you whether proofreading on paper or on a screen.

- Take a short break between writing and proofreading. Spending as little as five minutes on another task will help you a pproach the document with a fresheye.

- Read the text at least twice using a different method each time.
- Start at the top of the message. Read everything: not just text paragraphs but headings, footnotes, and so on.

- Read the text from bottom to top (word by word) to locate typographical and spelling errors.

- Read the text from bottom to top (sentence by sentence) to locate unclear structures.

- Read the text aloud from top to bottom, pointing to each word as you say it, to locate misspelled or misused words.

- If you are proofreading a document against an original copy, set the two side by side and compare them line by line, using envelopes or index cards to mark your place. When you are finished, read the finished document again by itself.

- Except where automatic numbering is used, check each set of numbered or lettered items individually to make sure the sequence is correct.

- Proofread numbers and technical data with a partner. The author of the document should read to the person who isn't familiar with the document.

- Watch for punctuation that comes in pairs (like parentheses); be sure both parts of the set are there.

- Proofread after every revision and editorial change. Be aware of the following errors associated with word-processed text:

- Duplication and missing transitions resulting from cutting and pasting.

- Editorial fragments resulting from trying various word combinations and forgetting to delete unwanted text.

**Figure 3-4**
Proofreading Tips

Spell checkers and grammar checkers are useful tools for proofreading, but they have limits. First, spell checkers will look only for errors in words listed in their dictionary. Second, spell checkers will not detect miskeyed words such as *form* for *from* or *good* for *food*. Contemporary word processing software will make some changes as you key (*teh* will appear as *the*), but these automatic changes are confined to commonly used words. Third, these tools often fail to recognize word choice errors such as *principle/principal*. (Appendix C, which contains a list of frequently confused words, is a useful resource for making word choice decisions.) Finally, grammar checkers will detect some errors but not others and sometimes suggest "corrections" that are incorrect.

For the best results, run the spell checker and grammar checker just before proofreading. Then check the document carefully yourself. Remember, software tools merely supplement good proofreading.

# CHAPTER SUMMARY

- Business writing is clear, complete, concise, and correct.

- Clarity involves word choice, unity, coherence, and structure.

- Choose words your receiver will understand.

- Write sentences and paragraphs that have one main idea.

- Use transitional words and phrases and repetition to link ideas.

- Add interest to your writing by using a variety of sentence structures.

- Be sure your messages include all the information the reader needs.

- Preserve clarity while striving for brevity. Limit repetition, eliminate excess words, emphasize verbs, and use the active voice.

- Make sure the content and mechanics of your message are accurate.

- Use a positive, unbiased, reader-centered tone.

- Take practical steps to overcome writer's block and draft your document.

- Focus on improving the content when revising a message.

- Focus on mechanics when editing a message.

- Make a final check of your finished document during proofreading.

- Revise, edit, and proofread as many times as necessary to produce a well-written message.

- Use spell checkers and grammar checkers as aids to proofreading, never to replace it.

# CHAPTER 3 APPLICATIONS

1. Find two simpler words for each of the following words. Use a dictionary or thesaurus as needed.

   a. acquiesce _____

   b. corroborate _____

   c. fruition _____

   d. gamut _____

   e. ludicrous _____

   f. mediocre _____

   g. queue _____

   h. reticent _____

   i. succumb _____

   j. whimsical _____

2. Find a specific way to describe each of the following vague terms and expressions.

   a. quick turnaround _____

   b. work late _____

   c. lucky _____

   d. computer _____

   e. keys fast _____

   f. software _____

   g. energy-efficient _____

   h. reliable _____

   i. excellent benefits _____

   j. holiday _____

3. For each of the following sentences, circle Y if the sentence has unity and N if it does not.

a.  Y    N    The café is popular among tourists, so be sure to make reservations.

b.  Y    N    It is cold in my office, so I need a new light fixture.

c.  Y    N    It was only 6 a.m. in Phoenix, but Bill phoned Karl to ask about the report.

d.  Y    N    While Martin was on vacation, Julia modified the database; Angie is ill today.

e.  Y    N    Three windows were broken during the storm; an insurance claim has been filed.

f.  Y    N    The security alarm is sounding; where do you plan to go during your vacation?

g.  Y    N    Follow the new guidelines when preparing your reimbursement request, and submit receipts for all meals over $10.

h.  Y    N    To take advantage of the discount, we must hire three new employees.

i.  Y    N    The temperature was so high this morning that I was able to walk barefoot in the park.

j.  Y    N    As you requested, the proposal will include a budget.

4. Form complete sentences by using transitional words or phrases to link the ideas in each of the following clauses. The type of transition to use is shown in parentheses.

a.  (cause/effect)          the budget will be cut by 3 percent          we can buy only two laptops

_____

b.  (time)                  drive north 3 miles                          turn right on Oak

_____

c.  (comparison)            online sales jumped 11 percent               in-store sales rose 11 percent

_____

d.  (sequence)              enter current data                           do a five-year comparison

_____

e.  (added information)     our company has good drivers                 it has excellent mechanics

_____

f.  (contrast)              I appreciate your thoughtfulness             I must refuse the invitation

_____

5. Rewrite the following sentences to make them brief.

    a.    When you hear the sound of the alarm, you must walk fast and leave the building.

    b.    After we have finished screening the materials we received from those who applied for the accounting position, we will conduct an interview with the top three candidates.

    c.    Because of the fact that Sabra is away and not available to represent us, the case will be handled by Robert.

    d.    There were only 50 people in the room when the meeting held during the month of May came to a close.

    e.    We want you to sign the form and send it back to us in the envelope that is enclosed with this letter.

    f.    When the CFO finished giving her financial presentation, the stockholders stood and clapped their hands together due to the fact that the company had performed well.

    g.    Adel has developed a low-cost, inexpensive procedure for us to use in place of the method we are using now for processing claims.

    h.    Michelle drew a perfectly round circle without using a compass or a pattern.

    i.    Kim and Andrea made similar suggestions about how we should solve the problem.

6. Rewrite the following sentences to eliminate the clichés.

    a.  Have a good day.

    b.  We must tighten our belts.

    c.  He's behaving like a fish out of water.

    d.  We will weather the storm.

    e.  Our backs are to the wall.

7. Rewrite the following sentences to eliminate dangling or misplaced modifiers and to correct problems with parallelism.

    a.  While traveling in Oregon, our car overheated.

    b.  Speaking from a worker's perspective, the keyboard should be lower.

    c.  The soap can be used to remove stains or for doing laundry.

    d.  You will find more products, faster checkout lines, and you will pay less.

    e.  The warranty only applies to the original buyer.

8. Rewrite the following sentences to emphasize the verb.

    a.   It is Kenneth's intention to resign at the end of the month.

    b.   Please conduct a thorough investigation and report your results by June 15.

    c.   Brenna gave a demonstration of the card reader for the customer.

    d.   Raul, Samantha, and Lynne had a discussion about office relocation.

    e.   Steven said he would make his decision by the end of the day.

9. Change the following sentences from the passive voice to the active voice.

    a.   The planning session was led by Marika Plante.

    b.   The machine has been repaired.

    c.   Dinner will be served at 7 p.m.

    d.   The package has been delivered to the loading dock.

    e.   The costume was designed by Margo Jago and sewn by Jack Perkins.

10. Change the following sentences from the active voice to the passive voice.

a. John Hazard wrote *The Munchkin Mystery*.

b. Julianne won the trip to Hawaii.

c. The clerk wrapped the package.

d. The mechanic replaced the water pump on the van.

e. The investment club donated $500 to the scholarship fund.

11. Rewrite the following sentences to make them more positive.

a. Don't hang your coat in the reception area closet.

b. You cannot use the photocopier until the toner cartridge has been replaced.

c. Your order cannot be processed until we receive your deposit.

d. People under age 18 are not eligible to enter the contest.

e. If you do not pay your membership dues, you will not receive the newsletter.

12. Rewrite the following sentences to reflect the reader's point of view or to create a neutral tone.

    a.   I appreciate your taking the time to interview me for the assistant manager position.

    b.   I'm going on vacation next week; you'll have to reschedule the meeting.

    c.   You damaged the camera when you dropped it.

    d.   We always like to have you send us comments and suggestions.

    e.   We cannot fill your order without a copy of your tax certificate.

13. Rewrite the following sentences to make them gender neutral.

    a.   Each candidate should submit his résumé and a letter of application.

    b.   Please have your salesman visit us early in March.

    c.   Six volunteers are needed to man the booth at next week's Business Expo.

    d.   Sylvia Sylvester, a female dentist, was nominated to be chairman of the awards committee.

    e.   The councilmen will vote on the issue next Monday.

14. Rewrite the following sentences to focus on people rather than their disabilities.

   a.   Although he is retarded, George is able to pull customer files with 95 percent accuracy.

   b.   The Freeport Flyers is a basketball team for people in wheelchairs.

   c.   Al, the epileptic groundskeeper, plans to open a nursery next spring.

   d.   The Most Valuable Player award was presented to Fran, a diabetic.

   e.   The public relations department recently hired a deaf artist.

15. Underline the correct term of those in parentheses. Use Appendix C as a resource.

   a.   We may not need the projector, but pack it (any way/anyway).

   b.   Nan, Margo, and Jerry will (come/go) to our home for dinner next Wednesday.

   c.   Jerry must decide (weather/whether) (farther/further) research would have a significant (affect/effect).

   d.   (Personal/Personnel) problems should be forgotten when the workday begins.

   e.   (Its/It's) the most important item on the (capital/capitol) improvement request.

   f.   Please check the shipment to (assure/ensure/insure) it is correct.

   g.   (Bring/Take) this package to the mail room.

   h.   Catalogs will be sent to (every one/everyone) on the preferred customer list.

   i.   Rocco (lead/led) visitors through the lobby and into the company store.

   j.   (Fewer/Less) people attended the meeting this year (than/then) attended last year.

16. Use the editing symbols shown in Appendix B to mark corrections and changes that are needed in the following document.

November 31, 200-

Ms. Suzanne Plotz
242 Starling Avenue
Martinsville, VA 24112-3833

Dear Mrs. Plotz

After receiving you're letter dated November 24, we conducted an investigation of your credit transactions for last month. The results appear below.

| October 3 | Men's Clothing | $119.40 |
| October 9 | Greeting Cards | 5.12 |
| October 18 | Women's Sportswear | 78.33 |
| | Shoes | 56.90 |
| | Men's Clothing (return) | −29.83 |
| October 23 | Housewares | 18.76 |
| October 29 | Boy's Clothing | 46.42 |
| November 6 | Linens | 27.86 |

According to our records, your purchases during the month of October totaled $295.10. The 15 percent discount applied to your account due to the fact that you are a you are a new credit card customer reduces the amount you owe to $259.69.

Ms. Plitz, please compare your charge slips with the transactions listed in this letter. If your records show the exact same amounts, please submit your payment by December 15. Otherwise, phone (276) 555-0175 too schedule an appointment with one of our customer service representatives.

Yours truly

Your Name

17. Exchange letters (Application 16) with another student in your class. Create a final version of the other student's message. Assume the letter will be printed on letterhead. Follow the guidelines for block letter style in Appendix A. Make only the corrections and changes that the other student has marked.

When your paper is returned, proofread it. If it is error-free, sign it; otherwise, mark the corrections that are needed and return it to your teammate. Repeat this process until the message is correct and ready to send.

18. Key the following document as a personal-business letter, referring to the guidelines for formatting personal-business letters in Appendix A. Make all the changes marked on the letter. Assume the role of the writer, Ailane P. Magnuson, 198 Cherry Street, Macon, GA 31201-3599. The receiver is Mr. Isaac Jarow, Vice President for Operations, RPB Corporation, Suite 34A, 297 River Bend Trail, Macon, GA 31211-9001. Use the current date.

---

Dear Mr. jarow


Thank your so much for speaking with me last Friday about the marketing position you have avail able at RPB Corporation it sounds fascinating. I especially like the fact that I would have an opportunity to use the sales training I received while enrolled as a student at Kragre Business School. As I mentioned during the interview, classes at Kragre end on Friday June 16 and I would be available to begin working the following weak. I'm looking forward to hearing from you. If I can provide you with additional information about my qualifications or experience, I will gladly do so.


Yours truly

---

# Writing Positive and Neutral News Messages

The United States Postal Service processes more than 200 billion pieces of mail annually. More than 50 million U.S. workers have access to e-mail. Americans fax about 70 million pages each year. Not all these messages are business communications, but the numbers are impressive—and data on instant messages and memos haven't been included! Faced with this level of competition, your messages must attract and hold your reader's attention to get the results you want. In this chapter, we'll explore how the direct approach is used to produce successful positive and neutral news messages.

## THE DIRECT APPROACH

The **direct approach** is used for messages the reader will view as neutral or favorable. The following types of messages use the direct approach:

- Requests
- Replies
- Informational messages

A message organized by the direct approach begins with the main idea, the purpose of the message. Putting the main idea first attracts attention and makes receivers want to read more. The supporting details follow in the next paragraph(s). After the necessary details are provided, the writer ends the message positively with a courtesy or action statement.

A good example of the direct approach is a traditional paper memo or an e-mail that announces the agenda for a meeting. The opening states the group's name and the time, day, date, and location of the meeting. Details about the items to be discussed, the order in which they will be handled, and who will be responsible for each would be considered supporting information. If the readers attend this meeting regularly, a goodwill statement such as *I'll look forward to seeing you at the meeting* is unnecessary. The content of the message will be received neutrally as a part of the reader's regular work. If the message were sent to a guest at the meeting, a forward-looking welcome would be fine.

### LEARNING OBJECTIVES

- Explain the direct organizational approach to writing messages.
- Compose effective requests for information or action.
- Write effective replies.
- Convey unsolicited informational messages clearly and completely.

*Put the main idea before the supporting details.*

The direct approach uses location and mechanics to create emphasis.

## Location

*Use location to emphasize important points.*

The first and last positions in a paragraph or message are emphatic. This means that readers notice text that appears in these places more than in other parts of a message. The **white space** surrounding each paragraph (the margins and the blank lines above and below) creates emphasis by giving readers a visual break between thoughts. The same effect is achieved when text is centered, indented, or introduced by a heading.

## Mechanics

*Font, type size, and display features also draw a reader's eye.*

Font, type size, and effects such as boldface and underscoring can be used to create emphasis. A vertical list with each item introduced by a number, letter, or symbol also highlights text. The points in a list are referred to as bullet points because they are targets for the reader's eye.

Writers must exercise restraint when using mechanical features to highlight text. When used to excess, mechanics can become a distracter rather than an attention-getter.

## [THINKING IT THROUGH 4-1]

## Benefits of Vertical Lists

Use a vertical list as you respond to the following questions:

1. In what ways does a vertical list help readers?

2. In what ways does a vertical list help writers?

# WRITING REQUESTS

The timely exchange of accurate information is essential in every organization, and request messages are the basis of these exchanges. Requests are received from and directed to customers, coworkers, or other organizations. The specific purpose of your requests can be to (1) ask for information or action, (2) place an order, or (3) make a claim.

Information/action requests and claims may be either direct or persuasive. Your analysis of the receiver's reaction will determine which strategy to use. When you think the reader will view the message positively or neutrally, use the direct approach. If you anticipate that the reader will need to be convinced to respond favorably, use the indirect approach. The direct approach is covered in this chapter; persuasion is covered in Chapter 6.

*Use the direct approach to organize routine requests.*

## Asking for Information or Action

Many of the messages you write on the job will be requests. You could send a memo or an e-mail to someone in another department asking for sales figures. You might write to a supplier asking for information about a product. You might inquire about a form or check that hasn't been received from a client. In your personal life, you might write to your insurance company about coverage for your computer equipment or ask a former teacher to give you a reference for a job. All these requests will have three parts: an opening, a middle, and a close.

### THE OPENING OF THE MESSAGE.

The opening is a clear statement of your request or a brief lead-in to it. For example, if you saw an ad offering a prospectus for a stock you might want to invest in, your opening might be *Please send me the investment prospectus for* . . . . In a message containing several specific questions, a good opening would be *Please provide the following information about* . . . . This courteous request would introduce a list of questions. Figure 4-1 shows a message that uses a numbered list.

*Begin with a specific request or a lead-in to it.*

### THE MIDDLE OF THE MESSAGE.

The middle clarifies the request or explains why you are making it. In this part of the message, you show how the reader will benefit from providing the information you ask for or by taking the action you request. If you use a list of questions, be sure they are written using clear, specific, parallel wording.

*Follow with supporting details or clarifying information.*

Make a conscious choice between asking close-ended questions (yes/no response) and open-ended questions (longer response). The question *What service contract length options are available?* will produce more information than the question *Is the service contract length variable?* Beware of close-ended questions that will yield a confusing or inadequate response. *Is your service contract fixed or variable?* may get an answer but will yield little useful information.

Be sure to provide all the information the reader will need to respond to the request.

TO:            Majorie Simmons, Administrative Assistant
               Research Department

FROM:          Edmund Crackle, Director    *ec*
               Human Resources Department

DATE:          June 1, 200-

SUBJECT:       Annual Performance Appraisal

Your annual performance review must be completed by June 30.  Please follow
these steps as you prepare for your review:

1.  Complete the attached form using your position description as a guide.
    Be specific about the tasks you perform and the portion of your time
    devoted to each task.

2.  Give the completed form to your supervisor by June 15.

3.  Make a one-hour appointment with your supervisor to discuss his/her
    evaluation of your performance. Allow at least ten days for him/her to
    complete the supervisor's portion of the form.

    During the meeting with your supervisor, you will be asked to sign the form.
    Your signature indicates that you have reviewed the appraisal. If you do not
    agree with the evaluation, you should submit a written rebuttal within ten
    calender days.  The review and your rebuttal, if you prepare one, will be
    placed in your personnel file.

    Our Personnel Evaluation Policy and a sample completed form are available
    on the Human Resources Department website (http://www.firstex.com/hr/
    policies); your employee number will serve as your password to enter the
    site. I'm available (Ext. 7982) if you have questions.

de

Attachment

c    R. K. Willoughby

## Figure 4-1
## Memo with Numbered List

> *Provide the details the reader needs to respond to the request.*

**THE CLOSE OF THE MESSAGE.**   The close provides details the reader needs to comply with the request. Is there a deadline by which you need a response? State it. Should the response be directed to someone else? Give the name and a complete mailing address, phone or fax number, or e-mail address. Express appreciation without using trite, overused, or outdated expressions such as *Thanking you in advance* or *If you have questions, please let me know.*

Analyze your receiver and the situation as you plan your message. These factors, together with your specific purpose, will help determine its length. Remember that the opening, middle, and close are parts of a message and can be developed as separate paragraphs or combined into one. The following internal e-mail message combines the opening, middle, and close in one brief paragraph:

What's our current inventory of MS-322s? I need the figure by noon for a report that must go out by 3 p.m. today. Thanks.

The message combines all the elements of good business writing: it is clear, complete, concise, and correct. In addition, it is courteous.

Messages written by individuals to organizations can be succinct, too, as shown in the following example:

Please remove information about me from all national direct mail and telemarketing lists maintained by your organization or its members.

Beginning the message with please makes the action a courteous request to be handled in a timely manner. The reader doesn't need to know why the writer wants to be removed from the list.

It would be unusual to have an external message as brief as either of the previous examples. An organization wouldn't want to risk creating a stark, impersonal image.

## Placing an Order

Most product or service orders are submitted on a seller's paper or online form. In some cases, the form is completed by the seller's representative during an on-site visit or a telephone call. If a blank form or the telephone number isn't available, send a letter. Make sure the letter contains all the information found on an order form:

- Item number
- Quantity
- Description
- Size
- Total cost
- Delivery destination
- Desired delivery date
- Color
- Unit cost
- Tax
- Shipping charges
- Payment method
- Contact information

Figure 4-2 on page 70 illustrates a complete order letter.

The opening to the order letter makes it clear that the writer is placing an order, not merely requesting information. The message gets right to the point and ends the same way. Appreciation is integrated into a sentence rather than being added as a separate statement.

**THE TREASURE CHEST**
809 Carey Avenue
Cheyenne, WY 82007-1311

February 10, 200-

Paxton Products Inc
PO Box 200
Mount Vernon, OR 97865-0200

Merchandise Order

Please ship the following music boxes and bill both product and shipping costs to
Account 354901-6.

| Item | Qty. | Description/Tune | Unit Price | Total Price |
|------|------|------------------|-----------|-------------|
| 245-RA | 7 | Rabbit/Here Comes Peter Cottontail | $7.49 | $52.43 |
| 245-CL | 3 | Sad Clowns/Send in the Clowns | $8.35 | $25.05 |
| 245-RO | 2 | Rosebud/Anniversary Waltz | $8.35 | $16.70 |

All items are from your spring catalog, which promises delivery within three weeks
for orders placed by February 15.

*Janice Gruder*

Janice Gruder
Manager

jn

**Figure 4-2**
Order Letter

## Making a Claim

Despite the good intentions and best efforts of everyone involved in
business transactions, things occasionally go wrong. Goods are damaged
during shipment, too few or wrong items are delivered, products don't
work, or service doesn't meet expectations. Research shows that happy
customers tell three friends, but unhappy customers tell nine. Businesses
recognize the importance of resolving customer relations problems
before sales are lost or the organization's image is damaged. Organizations view reasonable, timely claims as positive messages; therefore, use
the direct approach when writing them.

The opening to a claim is designed to capture the reader's attention and give an overview of the situation. The following sentence illustrates an effective opening statement:

Three of the chairs in the shipment delivered June 10 arrived with torn cushions.

When the remedy to the problem is obvious (replacement or reimbursement, for example), the desired action can be built into the opening:

Please ship three Model 374-G (ecru) posture chairs to replace the three damaged chairs delivered as part of the shipment received June 10.

Claims are good news.

Be clear from the start of a message that you are making a claim.

## [THINKING IT THROUGH 4-2]

## Controlling Anger, Part 1

Jordan Golden is angry and thinks he has a right to be. The MP3 player he ordered from a catalog arrived today, in time to be given to his sister on her sixteenth birthday, but not in gift condition. The case was cracked and the headset cord was frayed. Jordan has drafted what he thinks is an effective claim letter. You disagree and offer to help him revise the message. After reading what Jordan has prepared, write an appropriate **opening** for his claim.

Are you people in the business of selling used merchandise? It certainly seems that you are! I sent you $119.95 of my hard-earned money for what I thought would be a nice gift for my sister. Boy, was I wrong! I'll never do business with you people again. I want my money, an apology, and a new MP3 player. The sooner the better. Hattie's birthday is next week.

In the middle of the message, explain and document the claim. Describe the *who, what, when, where,* and *why* of the problem and *how* it was detected.

Stay calm and be objective. Your reader didn't cause the problem or observe what happened; your account must be a clear and honest description of the situation. If you're angry when you draft your claim letter, let several hours pass before you finalize and send it. When your anger subsides, you'll write a more effective message.

Use concrete terms. *Big gash* says less than *4″ × 1″ tear.* Enclose copies of purchase orders, invoices, shipping lists, proof of payment, or other documents related to the claim. Include photos of the damage if you have them. Put yourself in the reader's position. What would you need to know to respond positively to the claim?

## [ THINKING IT THROUGH 4-3 ]

## Controlling Anger, Part 2

Refer to the situation described in Thinking it Through 4-2. What information would you advise Jordan to include in the **middle** of his claim message?

If the action you want is not stated in the opening, you must describe it in the closing. Businesses appreciate writers who tell them what they want, as long as the request is reasonable. Threats (withholding business; publicizing the problem) or unreasonable demands (asking for a year's supply of water because one bottle in a 12-pack was empty) can make the reader defensive and unsympathetic to your claim.

Getting what you ask for may require information from the reader. In the close, you might ask what to do with damaged goods, how to return merchandise, and who will pay the shipping costs.

The closing also should build goodwill. Be gracious and sincere. Avoid overworked statements such as *Thank you for your prompt attention to this matter.*

A complete claim letter is shown in Figure 4-3. This message uses a subject line to introduce the topic and provide information related to the claim.

## THE TREASURE CHEST
809 Carey Avenue
Cheyenne, WY 82007-1311

March 10, 200-

Paxton Products Inc
PO Box 200
Mount Vernon, OR 97865-0200

Damaged Merchandise—Invoice 2312

Three of the twelve music boxes contained in the shipment received March 8 were broken.

When the package was delivered, our clerk noticed that one corner was crushed. The clerk commented about the condition of the package but was told by the carrier's representative that claims should be made to the shipper. When the clerk opened the box to examine its contents, he found the broken music boxes. Please replace the following merchandise:

| Item | Description/Tune | Condition |
|------|------------------|-----------|
| 245-CL | Sad Clown/Send in the Clowns | shattered |
| 245-RA | Rabbit/Here Comes Peter Cottontail | ear missing |
| 245-RO | Rosebud/Anniversary Waltz | petals cracked |

The damaged items are being returned to you c.o.d. We are confident that you will replace them by April 15 so that we will have them for our spring sale.

*Janice Gruder*

Janice Gruder
Manager

jn

**Figure 4-3**
Claim Letter

When you are disappointed with a product or service (personally or in the workplace), give the company a chance to correct the problem. Statistics show that fewer than half the people who have a valid complaint actually convey their disappointment or concerns to the company involved.

## Controlling Anger, Part 3

Review the situation described in Thinking it Through 4-2. Write the **closing** to the message.

---

WORKPLACE
CONNECTION

Promptly answered messages reflect the writer's good time-management skills.

*Message replies may be formal or informal.*

*Inquiry responses follow the direct approach: main idea, details, courteous close.*

# WRITING REPLIES

Every message that asks a question, makes a request, places an order, or makes a claim deserves a response, but not all responses need to be formal messages. A preprinted message form that says *This note is sent to facilitate a prompt reply* is one option. Another possibility is to stamp *Quick Reply* on the incoming letter or memo and write your response directly on the message. Reader analysis will help you determine whether informality is appropriate. If you use an informal method, make and retain a photocopy of the document before you send it.

When your analysis of the receiver and situation shows that a formal memo or letter is required, use the direct approach. This approach will serve you well as you write inquiry responses, request approvals, order acknowledgments or confirmations, and claim adjustments.

## Inquiry Responses

Begin your message with the information the writer wants or with a statement that introduces a vertical list of responses. Receiving the good news in the opening will encourage the receiver and motivate him or her to read the details. Do not use openings such as *Your letter regarding xxx has been received.* The reader knows this; why else would you be writing?

In the middle of the message, give complete responses to questions the reader has asked. Don't add unnecessary details; it wastes your time and could annoy the reader. If a shipment is late because of a factory fire, the reader doesn't care about where the factory is located, when the fire took place, or other details. The reader only wants to know when the shipment will be delivered.

End with a courteous, forward-looking statement that sounds fresh and sincere. *Write again if we can help on a future project* is better than *If you have additional questions, please do not hesitate to contact us.* The letter in Figure 4-4 presents one possible response to a letter asking for information about a potential vacation destination.

Use fresh, sincere wording in the close.

---

**Bangor Tourism Office**
10 Cumberland Place • Bangor, ME 04401-5085
1-800-555-0110 • info@bangortourist.gov

March 10, 200-

Mr. Blake Amroke
5768 East Seventh Avenue
Monroe, LA 71201-3371

Dear Mr. Amroke

As you requested, we are enclosing the following items:

- Maps for the city of Bangor and the downtown area.

- A brochure that lists several area lodging facilities and the amenities they offer.

- Brochures describing parks, recreational facilities, shopping, and cultural sites in Bangor and Penobscot County.

- A list of special events occuring in our area during June and July.

Our office is located in downtown Bangor—we've marked it for you on the map. Stop in during your visit, and we'll tell you more about the area. You may also wish to consult our website at the adress below. There you'll find links to sites describing more of what this area has to offer you and your family.

We're looking forward to sharing the beauty of Maine with you this summer.

Sincerely

*Adeline Wilcox*

Adeline Wilcox, Tourism Director

Enclosures

Visit our website at http://www.bangortourist.gov.

**Figure 4-4**
Inquiry Response

# Request Approvals

Approve requests by presenting the good news first: *Yes! You and your Junior Achievement group may tour our production facility on October 29.* The pleasure associated with knowing the request has been approved will motivate the reader to learn what must be done next.

The middle of the message gives important information. The detail section should be clear and complete. If details are unclear, the reader won't understand. If details are incomplete, additional communication will be needed. A positive close comes after the details.

# Order Acknowledgments or Confirmations

Because customers are more interested in receiving their merchandise than in reading about their order, acknowledgments and confirmations are not always sent. This is especially true for direct mail businesses that have many one-time customers or repeat customers who buy infrequently. When organizations do acknowledge orders, a preprinted card or a computer-generated card or e-mail is convenient. The acknowledgment may list the items and the shipping date or may consist simply of a statement such as *Your order is being prepared for shipment; you should receive it within two weeks.*

Special circumstances call for a formal response. The first order from a new customer, a large order from a regular customer, a shipment that must be delayed, or an order that can't be filled completely are examples of special circumstances that require a formal response.

E-mail has become popular for customer service communication. To ensure it's effective, Marilynne Rudick and Leslie O'Flahavan of **E-WRITE**, authors of Clear, Correct, Concise E-Mail: A Writing Workbook for Customer Service Agents, recommend that organizations avoid the following errors:

1. **Failing to respond**. Unanswered e-mail suggests you don't want the customer's business.

2. **Sending a form response that doesn't fit the situation.** Form messages can be efficient, but they are effective only when they fit the situation. A "canned" response that doesn't answer the writer's question implies you didn't understand it or chose to ignore it.

3. **Using a website as a default response.** Answer the customer's question in your e-mail; don't send him or her to the website for the answer. You can refer the writer to the website for additional information, but be specific—give the page URL.

4. **Ignoring opportunities to build goodwill.** Every response should make a customer feel valued.

5. **Sending a sloppy response.** Spelling and grammar errors cast doubt on the company's ability to perform its core business activities accurately.

**Figure 4-5**
E-mail in Customer Service

If an order acknowledgment or confirmation has good and bad news, use the direct approach and present the good news first. Tell the reader what will be delivered on time, explain why some items will be delivered late, and stress when the reader can expect to receive the late shipment. Placing the explanation in an introductory dependent clause helps emphasize the good news in the independent clause that follows. *Although floods in the Red River Valley have temporarily halted production of the Rapid Cut 330 in our region, your order is receiving priority at our West Region plant. Your shipment should reach you by May 1.*

Mixed-news messages use the direct approach, with the good news first.

**Resale** or **promotional** information can be added to order acknowledgments and confirmations. Resale statements highlight one or two of the product's features or reassure readers that their purchase was a good one. Promotional statements describe new or related products and services.

Promotional or resale material may be incorporated into a reply message.

The closing of an acknowledgment letter expresses appreciation and a desire to continue the business relationship. *We appreciate the confidence you have in us, Mrs. Whitehall. You can always count on our high-quality products and reliable service.*

## [THINKING IT THROUGH 4-5]

## Acknowledging an Order

The sporting goods company for which you work recently implemented an online order processing system. Your task is to write a brief statement that will be sent electronically to the e-mail address supplied by the purchaser.

1.  What items should you include in the acknowledgment?

2.  Write the acknowledgment, using an underscore (_____) where variable information would be inserted.

## Claim Adjustments

Claims help organizations provide better products and services.

Businesses have ethical and legal obligations to make adjustments for valid claims against their products and services. However, it is not the fear of legal action that encourages businesses to process claims efficiently and effectively. It is the desire to serve their customers. Good customer service can produce repeat business. Handling claims to the satisfaction of customers leads to good word-of-mouth advertising. Furthermore, paying attention to customer feedback can lead to better products or services.

So much is gained by adjusting claims satisfactorily that businesses do so routinely. Most medium-to-large firms have consumer affairs or customer relations departments to handle the task. Unless a claim is clearly bogus or the requested adjustment is outrageous, companies usually will settle the claim quickly and happily.

Claim adjustment messages are often form letters. The core of each message is filed electronically and then retrieved and personalized for the customer and the situation. Figure 4-6 shows a completed claim adjustment form letter.

The letter uses the direct approach: The opening says what claim is being adjusted, the middle gives details and tries to restore customer confidence, and the close encourages repeat business.

Choose words carefully; avoid apologies unless absolutely necessary.

Most writers believe apologies do more harm than good because they can be construed as an admission of guilt. If used late in the message, apologies remind the reader of the problem and diminish goodwill.

© 1998 Ted Goff

"We told you we were coming. Didn't you read our memo?"

November 27, 200-

Ms. Kelly Raitt
1401 N. Lark Street
Weatherford, OK 73096-2702

Dear Ms. Raitt

Thank you for telling us about your experience with Bailey's Blueberry Muffin Mix. You deserve the highest-quality products when you buy Bailey's, and we strive to be sure you get them.

Our Quality Assurance staff has examined the material you sent and has identified it as residue from a blueberry plant leaf.

Because of the rigid quality control standards we set, we are concerned when materials other than our high-quality ingredients find their way into our products. You may be assured that we will take steps to prevent similar incidents from occurring in the future.

Please accept the enclosed coupons as a token of our appreciation for your interest in keeping the quality of Bailey's mixes high. We trust that you will try our products again and find them to be delicious and convenient.

Sincerely

*Melvin Patronas*

Melvin Patronas
Consumer Affairs Manager

jt

Enclosures

PO Box 572 | Overland Park, KS | 66201-0572
(913) 555-0170 | http://www.coarcompany.com

## Figure 4-6
Claim Response

Tone and word choice are very important in adjustment letters. The tone must be polite, not condescending. The situation must be explained without placing blame. Confidence should be restored without promising that the situation will never happen again.

# WRITING UNSOLICITED INFORMATIONAL MESSAGES

Many of the messages distributed within an organization are unsolicited. Their purpose is to inform rather than to respond to questions or requests. These messages, sent as e-mails or memos, provide information needed for work to be done; explain events, policies, and procedures; or deliver other work-related information. Because informational messages are routine, writers expect readers to have a neutral or positive reaction. The messages are, therefore, organized by the direct approach. The following text, sent by e-mail, is an example:

> Two early morning power surges caused a loss of long-distance telephone service. We expect to have the switch repaired by noon today.

Informational messages also can be sent to external audiences. Office relocations, deadline extensions, calls for bids and proposals, routine billing notices, and reports from subcontractors to contractors illustrate some of these communications.

---

**This passage from a business memo was printed in the "Doublespeak" feature of *The Winner's Circle*.**

"A spot-check of randomly selected directories indicated that a number of the directories contained several blank pages. In view of the foregoing it is suggested that each user review the issued directory and ascertain whether or not the directory is complete. In the event the directory is incomplete, the user should return the directory to issue source for disposition."

*Translation*: If your directory has blank pages, send it back to me.

---

# CHAPTER SUMMARY

- Use the direct approach when you expect readers will have a positive or neutral reaction to your message.
- The direct approach has the following parts:

  1. An opening that focuses on the main idea—the purpose of the message.
  2. A middle that provides details to support the main idea.
  3. A positive close, with a courtesy or action statement that generates goodwill.

- Use the direct approach when writing requests, replies, and informational messages.
- Requests are made to ask for information, place an order, or make a claim.
- Replies consist of inquiry responses, request approvals, order acknowledgments or confirmations, and claim adjustments.
- Unsolicited informational messages provide information needed for work to be done; explain events, policies, or procedures; or deliver other work-related information.

*Chapter 4:  Writing Positive and Neutral News Messages*

## Section I: Work-Related Messages

The following exercises require you to apply the direct approach in writing work-related messages. Read the directions carefully. Unless your instructor tells you otherwise, use the style you prefer for memos or letters (several styles are presented in Appendix A). Begin letters with the date (no return address is needed). Send e-mails to your instructor. Use today's date unless another date is given, and create reasonable details as necessary. Apply the 4Cs of communication that you learned about in Chapter 3, and remember to proofread your message for mechanics.

1. You manage the chemical stockroom at Enterprise Pharmaceuticals. Chemicals are purchased and stored centrally. Departments are billed for whatever they use. It is your job to tell employees that on the first of next month the stockroom hours will change from 1–3 p.m. to 9–11 a.m. Most of Enterprise's shipments arrive in the afternoon, and shifting the stockroom hours will allow your staff to do an inventory and shelve the new stock without interruption. You're willing to fill requests that arrive in the afternoon, but a 15 percent markup will be added.

   Plan your communication by answering the following questions:

   a. Who will read your message?

   b. Through what medium will you distribute the message? Why did you select this method?

   c. What is the main idea?

   d. What details must you include?

   e. Are readers required to reply? If so, how? By when?

   f. What positive thought would you use to close the message?

   g. Are enclosures needed? If so, what?

   Using the notes you made in items a–g, write the message at the top of the next page.

*continued on next page* ▼

Write your message here:

2. When you arrived at work this morning, you found a note from your supervisor (Suzanne Samkoff, Office Services Department Manager) asking you to "Finish, edit, add my initials, and send this. We need to know how many they want and where to deliver them. You'll process the requests as we receive them." Do as Suzanne asks.

All Admin. Support Staff

The new edition of the corporate style manual has arrived! The manual offers the latest, newest information about the letter, punctuation, memo, and envelope styles used here at Tibot Industries. It also dispenses priceless information about in-house reprographics services and proposes numerous suggestions on how we can economize—time and dollars. How can YOU get a copy of this worthwhile

3. The "Tidbits" section of the March issue of *Today's Technology* contained the following item:

SCZ has announced a new program that automates the scheduling process. Users input their staffing needs for each hour of the week. MORETIME matches them to worker lists and produces a schedule. One Chicago clothing store that used the system cut overstaffed hours by 85 percent and reduced understaffed hours by 58 percent. After just two weeks of testing, managers refused to schedule manually any longer.

You manage the home furnishings department of Old Oak Department Store. You believe MORETIME would benefit your store. After reading "Tidbits," you phoned a local computer store to ask about the software. The clerk said the store didn't stock MORETIME and that she wasn't familiar with it. She was able, however, to tell you that SCZ's mailing address is 223 W. Katella Avenue, Anaheim, CA 92802-3603. Prepare an appropriate message.

4. Refer to Application 3. SCZ has responded to your request. Old Oak's department managers meet the second Tuesday of each month. The store manager sets the agenda for department managers' meetings. You'd like the group to spend 10 to 15 minutes discussing the possibility of buying the software. Prepare and send an appropriate e-mail to the manager (your instructor).

5. You manage the Half Note Music Store, 163 Chestnut Street, Philadelphia, PA 19106-3017, (215) 555-0148, http://www.halfnotemusic.com. The owner has asked you to prepare a flyer that could be distributed to customers to announce a special Valentine's Day promotion—That Special Song." The owner wants people to share stories of their "special song—its title, the name of the artist who performed it, and how it became special. The author of the best story will receive a dozen roses and a $75 certificate for dinner at a local restaurant. All those who submit stories will have their names entered in a drawing for three free CDs. The deadline for entries is February 10.

6. Refer to Application 5. The Valentine's Day promotion was a success. More than 150 entries were received. You believe, and the owner concurs, that it would be good to send all participants a list of who won and enclose a certificate for 10 percent off their next purchase. Prepare the message.

7. Your supervisor has asked you to notify the members of the budget committee that the meeting scheduled for 10 a.m. next Monday has been rescheduled for 2 p.m. on Thursday of the following week. The site has also changed to Room 312. The change is because of a delay in getting a tax ruling from the Internal Revenue Service. No new items will be added to the agenda. Write the message and e-mail it to your instructor.

8. Your company has decided to issue photo ID badges to its employees. Effective June 1, employees must show their badge to gain entry to areas beyond the lobby. Your supervisor has given you the job of coordinating the photo sessions.

   a. Prepare a message to be sent to the employees of your firm. Cameras will be set up in Conference Room A from 8:30 a.m. to 4 p.m. each weekday from May 1 to May 12. Appointments aren't necessary. Workers should bring a completed information card with them. Badges will be distributed by the end of the month.

   b. It's April 25. Prepare a message to the department secretaries in your company asking them to remind workers about the photo sessions. Send your message to your instructor.

   c. Write to the photographer, Paul Peterson, 308 N.E. Fifth Avenue, Boca Raton, FL 33432-4059, to confirm the sessions. When you spoke with him last week, Paul said he preferred to leave his equipment in or near the room where photos are to be taken. There's a closet in the conference room. The closet and the room can be locked each evening. He may leave his equipment there, but you assume no liability for damage or theft.

9. You work for a major insurance company. Your task is to prepare a message telling policyholders about a new program. If they are or become a member of a participating health club (enclose a list) and exercise at least ten times a month, policyholders will be reimbursed for $25 of the club's monthly membership fee. Policyholders should bring your message and a copy of their health-care membership card to the club and complete forms available there. They must provide a voided check or savings account deposit slip to facilitate the reimbursement process. The club is responsible for submitting monthly reports and certifying that individuals have exercised the required number of times. The offer will continue indefinitely; participants will receive 60-day notice before termination.

10. As bookkeeper for your company, you are concerned about a bill received from Amrika Cleaning Service (184 Bear Hill Road, Waltham, MA 02451-1036). Last month, your firm contracted with Amrika to vacuum your office with HEPA vacuum cleaners. The contract you signed was for labor and materials, but the bill you received also lists $45 for "subsistence." You object to paying for dinner for the workers and want the unauthorized charge removed from your bill. Prepare an appropriate message.

11. The department store where you are employed routinely prints coupons in the newspaper. In the past, the coupons could be applied to regular, sale, and clearance merchandise. Starting the first of next month, the coupons will no longer apply to clearance merchandise. The coupons will reflect the change but, as manager, you want to be sure your sales associates know about it and are prepared to respond to customers who didn't notice the change. Prepare an appropriate message.

12. Last night, you had a business dinner at a local restaurant. The table service and the food quality were fine, but you were disappointed with the atmosphere. When not serving other patrons, the wait staff gathered by the door to the kitchen and chatted. Clearly, they were in a good mood because their laughter would occasionally overshadow the conversation at your table. Because the worst interruptions occurred near the end of your dinner, you didn't say anything to the server. Now, though, you believe the manager should know of your disappointment. Prepare an appropriate message (William's on the River, 600 Decatur Street, New Orleans, LA 70310-1011).

13. You are the customer service representative at Rapid Copy Printers. Yesterday you received a letter from a regular customer, Storey Cabinets, with this message:

OOPS!

Three of the twelve boxes of envelopes delivered March 15 (Invoice No. 18664-2) contained the incorrect logo and return address.

When the order arrived, our clerk opened one box and checked the first envelope for accuracy. Finding no problem, the clerk signed the receipt and shelved the boxes. Today, when the envelopes were distributed to users, we noticed that two of the boxes contained envelopes bearing the logo and return address of Chaffee Investments. A sample is enclosed.

Please send us two boxes of envelopes imprinted with our logo and return address. Also, let us know what you would like us to do with Chaffee's envelopes.

Write a response to Mark Noyes, Purchasing Agent for Storey (537 Chiricahua Avenue, Douglas, AZ 85607-2868), approving the claim. Chaffee's envelopes should be destroyed. Two boxes of correctly imprinted envelopes should reach Storey Cabinets by March 30. Two desk calendars will be included in the shipment at no charge. Use March 23 for the date.

14. Your office has a "sunshine" fund. The money pays for cards and flowers sent to workers to recognize occasions such as weddings, births, graduations, illnesses, or deaths. After paying the bill you received today, you have only $14.95 in the fund. It's time to ask for contributions for the coming year. Prepare a message to be circulated to the 30 people in your office. (Would it be appropriate to suggest a minimum amount?)

15. You are a sales associate in a furniture store that stocks expensive merchandise. A lamp, for example, could cost as much as $500. Each sale generates a commission for you. Prepare a form letter to customers who make purchases from you. Personalize this message so these customers will ask for you the next time they shop at your store.

16. Beth and Ben Hilager (2618 Poplar Springs Drive, Meridian, MS 39305-4613) have asked your company to sponsor the local youth soccer team they coach. Sponsorship includes paying a $75 league entry fee and furnishing printed T-shirts for the players. If you sponsor a team, you can choose a name for it. You know from experience that some sponsors also contribute money toward post-game refreshments and an end-of-season banquet. Prepare an appropriate response to the request.

17. You prepare taxes in an accounting firm. Each spring, as you get ready for the tax season, you send your clients a worksheet that outlines the figures you used to prepare their taxes the previous year. If clients take the time to complete the worksheet showing their income and expenses for the current tax year, the billable time devoted to preparing their taxes will be greatly reduced. Prepare a form letter urging your clients to complete and return the worksheet promptly.

18. You are an insurance agent. Last night, your area was struck by a tremendous storm. The three-inch rainfall was bad enough, but the 40 mph winds and baseball-size hail were the real problem. Many of your policyholders' homes and cars were damaged. You've worked with your regional office and identified four contractors who will work with you to do home repair estimates. In addition, you've arranged to have a satellite auto assessment center established in the parking lot of a local office building. Write a form letter to your clients providing them with appropriate information.

19. E-mail everyone in your company to inform them that one of two elevators in the west wing will undergo routine maintenance next Monday; the other, the Monday after. Work will be done during regular business hours and should take no more than one day.

20. You recently began work as a travel planner for a medium-sized consulting firm. Your predecessor created profiles for each consultant who used your service, but you've found that some of the information in those profiles is inaccurate. Therefore, you've decided to ask your clients to verify the information. Prepare a form message to be attached to the profile you will send each traveler.

21. Your company prepares both print and online telephone directories for use by employees. The print directories are distributed in June, but the online directory is updated as changes occur. It's January 12. Barbara Jasper will retire as head of the accounting department at the end of this month, and Ced Ivy will replace her. Prepare an e-mail to the communications department notifying them of the change.

22. Refer to Application 21. It's now February 8. You've been getting mail and calls directed to Barbara Jasper. When you check the online directory, you see that Barbara Jasper is still listed as head of your department. Send a follow-up e-mail to the communications department.

23. Refer to Applications 21 and 22. Assume the role of administrative assistant in the communications department and respond to the e-mail sent in Application 22. Thom Ryelts, who maintains the online directory, has been on medical leave following surgery; he's expected to return February 20 and will take care of the backlog of changes then.

# Section II: Personal-Business Messages

The following exercises relate to using the direct approach in writing situations you might face in your personal life. Read the directions carefully. Use the personal-business letter format (refer to Appendix A). Use today's date, and invent reasonable details as necessary. Apply the 4Cs of good communication presented in Chapter 3. Plan before you write, and proofread for mechanics.

24. The Business Leaders of Tomorrow club at the high school you attended has invited you to speak at its annual awards banquet on May 12. They want you to give a 15-minute presentation on a topic of your choice. The event will be held in the Empire Room of the Imperial Hotel. Dinner will be served at 7 p.m., and the program will begin at 8. Your spouse or a guest may also attend. Convey your acceptance to Geoff Tubbs, chair of the Program Committee.

25. When you bought a new portable telephone/answering machine unit last month, you saved money by taking the display unit for a discontinued model. Unfortunately, the clerk couldn't find the instruction manual. You would like a copy of the manual to be sure you are getting the full benefit of the unit. You stopped at the store, and the clerk advised you to write to the manufacturer (TuneIn Company, 114 Main Street, Williston, ND 58801-6018). Prepare an appropriate message.

26. You and two friends spent last weekend in Chicago. You arrived home late Sunday night, unpacked your suitcase, and discovered that your travel alarm was missing. You realized you must have left it on the bedside table in your hotel room. You phoned the hotel (Sandburg Hotel, 32 West Adams Street, Chicago, IL 60603-5501) but were unable to learn whether the clock had been found. The desk clerk advised you to write to Ramona DeAngeles, housekeeping supervisor for the hotel. Do as the clerk advised.

27. You got home from work late last night and weren't in the mood to cook a full meal, so you decided to prepare a salad and a box of macaroni and cheese. When you opened the box, you found pasta but no cheese. Frustrated, you ordered a pizza and vowed that today you would write to the company. Write an appropriate claim message (TasteRite, Inc., 1973 Roebuck Drive, Meridian, MS 39301-6633).

28. You are a member of several clubs and professional associations. Prepare the text of a message notifying these groups that you are moving six weeks from today. Your new address is 52 Holly Street, Denver, CO 80220-5859. Your telephone number is (303) 555-0147.

29. You are looking for a new job. Prepare a message asking a current or former teacher or employer to be a reference for you.

30. The mystery novel you ordered from an online distributor arrived yesterday, and you began reading it last night. As the plot thickened, you turned the page and found . . . nothing! The next four pages were blank. Return the book and ask for a replacement (Carpathia Books, 486 Thomas Street, Seattle, WA 98109-4621).

# Writing Bad News Messages

Citizens of Austria were very proud when one of their own, Elfriede Jelinek, won the 2004 Nobel Prize for literature. The Austrian post office offered to place a likeness of the author on a postage stamp. Being honored in this manner is quite rare. In the United States, for example, prominent people (with the exception of former Presidents) are eligible for such commemoration only ten years after their death. The novelist and playwright declined, saying she sought "no personal honours." The decision was certainly a disappointing one for postal officials, but they very likely respected Ms. Jelinek for the candor with which she explained her refusal.

## TYPES OF BAD NEWS MESSAGES

Bad news messages can be classified into three types—*request refusals*, *adjustment refusals*, and *unexpected bad news*. Request and adjustment refusals are written in response to messages from customers, employees, or others. Unexpected bad news arises from decisions made within an organization. These decisions must be conveyed to those affected by them.

## THE INDIRECT APPROACH

Most people dislike giving bad news almost as much as they dislike receiving it. Nevertheless, bad news is a reality in business. Because bad news can't be avoided, writers usually soften it by using the indirect approach.

### Why the Indirect Approach Works

The **indirect approach** is based on psychology. It draws on an understanding of how receivers generally respond to the arrangement and wording of important information in a message. Specifically, this approach applies psychology with regard to *location*, *space*, *reading patterns*, and *acceptance versus pleasure*.

LOCATION. Writers know that the first and last positions in a paragraph or message have the greatest emphasis. Therefore, they do not put bad news in either location. If the bad news appeared first, a receiver might not read the entire message. Yet, the rest of the message contains important information about *why* the news is bad. If the bad news ends the message, it overshadows the explanation.

**SPACE.**   People equate space with importance. The more space devoted to an idea, the more important it will seem. Writers minimize bad news by limiting it to one sentence or to a clause within a sentence. Because it is emphatic, however, writers do not use a single-sentence paragraph to present bad news.

**READING PATTERNS.**   Writers know that people tend to start at the top of a message and will read to the end only if their interest can be held. By delaying their presentation of the bad news, writers hold the interest of their readers.

**ACCEPTANCE VERSUS PLEASURE.**   Writers acknowledge that readers may never *like* receiving bad news. Therefore, they try to get receivers to *accept* that they were treated fairly and that the decision was not arbitrary or mean-spirited. When acceptance occurs, the relationship between the sender and the receiver will stay strong and goodwill will be retained.

## Parts of Indirect Bad News Messages

A bad news message organized by the indirect approach has five sections: *buffer, explanation, bad news, counterproposal/resale*, and *close*. Bad news is placed in the middle of the message. The placement is strategic, not deceptive. The following paragraphs describe the sections of an indirect bad news message.

**THE BUFFER.**   Bad news messages begin with a buffer. A **buffer** is a statement related to the *topic* of the message but unrelated to the bad news. It engages the reader without indicating whether good or bad news follows. The buffer softens the impact of the bad news.

A buffer may be positive or neutral. Positive buffers are used when some aspect of the situation is favorable. For example, a positive buffer would be used when part of an order can be delivered and part will be delayed. If no part of the order is available, the buffer would be neutral.

A buffer should be brief. A long buffer may suggest that the writer is avoiding something and may make the reader suspicious.

A good buffer does not indicate whether a request is being approved or denied. It contains an apology only when the writer is at fault. Here's an example:

> Your October 7 letter describing the problem you are having with your Springer Lawn Trimmer has been referred to me. I apologize for not responding to your letter sooner.

In this buffer, the writer is apologizing for not responding quickly, not for the request denial that will come later. The difference is subtle, but important. Note, too, that the writer did not thank the receiver for his or her message. Gratitude should be used sparingly and cautiously in bad news messages because its meaning could be misinterpreted.

Buffers should not mislead the reader. Suppose an account representative, trying to be positive, writes to a customer, "Thank you for your letter regarding the problems you have been experiencing with your MP3 player. We are committed to providing you with excellent service." This pleasant opening builds the reader's confidence that good news follows. When the reader learns the request has been denied, he or she may be confused or may become angry and disregard the explanation—that the warranty expired the year before.

> Don't mislead your reader, intentionally or unintentionally.

## [ THINKING IT THROUGH 5-1 ]

## Analyzing Buffers

Are the following buffers strong or weak? Why?

1. Thank you for your memo, Maxine; it's always a pleasure to hear from a hard-working, loyal employee.

2. The clothing you returned has obviously been worn. We're surprised you tried to return it for credit.

3. Seung, it was good to get your e-mail. It's been quite a while since we in Payroll have heard from you or any of the other people in the Safety Division. I hear you've put together a strong team for this year's summer softball league!

4. As you requested, your video camera has been checked. Our technicians have determined that the camera requires a minor adjustment and replacement of only one part.

A good buffer introduces the topic without revealing the bad news and forms a natural bridge to what follows—an explanation or reasons for the bad news.

## THE EXPLANATION.

The explanation is usually the longest part of the message. In this section, the writer clearly and honestly presents information designed to get the reader to accept the bad news that will follow.

As you prepare the transition from the buffer to the explanation, choose your words carefully. Transitional words such as *unfortunately* and *however* signal a change from the positive or neutral tone of the opening and may make the reader defensive before he or she reads the explanation. Another word to avoid is *but*. Think about how you feel when you ask someone to do something and the response is, "I'd like to help you, but . . ." Your reader will experience the same disappointment.

© 2000 Ted Goff

## "Please take this memo to Mr. Stanfield and tell me how many things he throws at you after he reads it."

A good explanation shows how this specific reader, or customers or employees in general, benefit from the policy that was the basis for the decision. For example, the statement *Participants are guaranteed personal attention when the trainer:student ratio is held at 12:1* shows concern for providing a high-quality learning environment. An explanation such as *We can't afford to offer a flexible spending account* is writer-centered and money-focused. An explanation such as *It's against our policy to provide cash refunds* is unclear. Weak explanations can make readers resentful. What is the policy? Why does it exist? Be specific.

Only one *good* reason is required. Include additional reasons if they will increase goodwill and help the reader accept the bad news without destroying the brevity of the message. Stretching for reasons can weaken the explanation. As part of the planning process, the writer should list and prioritize the reasons for saying no. If the reasons cannot be listed or if they are not convincing, reevaluate the negative decision or action.

*The explanation presents your reasons.*

**Receiver benefit is a theme often used by retail and other businesses when they engage in repair or remodeling projects that could inconvenience their customers. Prominently placed signs with wording such as *Remodeling to serve you better* put a positive spin on the situation and frame it from the customer's perspective.**

Be careful, too, not to insult the reader. Condescending language such as *Surely you understand, You claim,* or *We have never had a request like this before* will make the reader defensive.

*Respect your receiver.*

## [THINKING IT THROUGH 5-2]

## Receiver Benefit

Explain how receivers benefit from each of the following policies:

1. A custodial firm will raise the hourly cost of its service by 25 cents because it is converting to environmentally friendly cleaning equipment and supplies.

2. A company will not provide ATM passwords by phone.

By the time the receiver has read the buffer and the explanation, he or she should be prepared for, and not be surprised by, what follows—the bad news.

**THE BAD NEWS.** Bad news may be implied or expressed. **Implied** bad news hints at the *no*. **Expressed** bad news is more specific. If you must use negative words, choose them carefully. Be tactful, not blunt. Base your choice of implied or expressed bad news on your analysis of the receiver. In general, implied bad news is preferred. Notice in the following example that the same bad news can be implied or expressed.

Implied:     Paid leaves of absence are available only to employees who have been with the company for one year or more.

Expressed:  Paid leaves of absence are available only to employees who have been with the company for a year or more. Because you began working at Goodhue only three months ago, you are not yet eligible for a paid leave of absence.

## [ THINKING IT THROUGH 5-3 ]

## Implied Bad News

Marie Bluskin, owner of Marie's Cards and Gifts, has submitted an order for ten figurines and has asked you to apply your usual quantity discount to her purchase. This is Marie's first purchase from your firm, and you would like to keep her as a customer. You offer a 15 percent quantity discount, but only on purchases of 50 or more figurines. Draft two bad news statements, one using the implied approach and the other using the expressed approach. Decide which you would prefer to use in a letter, and explain why.

Implied Bad News:


Expressed Bad News:


Choice and Explanation:


Recall from the discussion of psychology earlier in this chapter that a one-sentence paragraph is emphatic. Since writers want to minimize the emphasis on the bad news, they often link it to the explanation or to the counterproposal/resale section.

## The Counterproposal/Resale.

The **counterproposal** is one of the most important sections of a bad news message. It is the place where the writer shows genuine concern for and interest in helping the receiver. It is where the writer says, "I can't do what (or everything) you ask, but here's what I will do." The counterproposal should be reasonable, as in this example:

> Although Model 381 is no longer available, Model 382 has the same features—and more!

Offer reasonable alternatives.

The counterproposal should be stated positively and clearly. It should include all the details the reader needs to take action. Provide names, addresses, phone numbers, dates, costs, figures, and other information; include a reply card or brochure as appropriate. Make the communication as complete as possible.

As previously noted, writers often try to minimize the impact of bad news by linking it to the explanation or to the counterproposal/resale section. When linked to the counterproposal, the bad news is typically presented in a dependent clause. Here is an example:

> Although your practical work experience is too limited for you to become a finalist for the accounts manager position, the accounts associate position we have available seems to suit you well. The position calls for a self-motivated, energetic person who has at least one year of postsecondary accounting education and familiarity with information systems.

**Resale** is used in situations where a counterproposal is impossible or impractical. Resale material is designed to restore, maintain, or build goodwill between the sender and the receiver. For example, a message to scholarship applicants who were not selected to receive an award doesn't offer an opportunity for a counterproposal. A statement or two about some particular strength of the candidate's background would be appropriate. The statement(s) would be considered resale because they make the reader feel good about himself or herself and about the scholarship organization. Here is an example:

Resale can restore, maintain, or build goodwill.

> The selection committee was very impressed by your career goals and your strong work experience. You can be proud of your accomplishments.

Coupons or discounts on future purchases are additional examples of resale. If neither a counterproposal nor resale material is appropriate, include additional reasons for the decision. Any of the three will help minimize the bad news. Once this section has been presented, it is time to close the message.

## The Close.

Because the last position in a message is emphatic, writers should end bad news messages with a positive, friendly close.

### Workplace Connection

If you have difficulty finding the right words to write bad news messages, try to visualize your reader and speak as though she or he were seated beside you. Then, write what you said.

Any reference to the bad news, no matter how well-meaning the writer may be, merely reminds the receiver about it. Referring to the bad news defeats the efforts that went into de-emphasizing it.

The **close** may relate to the reader, the counterproposal, or the business relationship between the sender and the receiver—anything that is on the topic but *off* the bad news. Choose words carefully. Avoid words that show doubt (*hope, if* ) and words that are negative (*problem, condition, situation*).

[ **THINKING IT THROUGH 5-4** ]

## Closings

Are the following closings strong or weak? Why?

1. Please do not hesitate to call if you encounter this problem again.

2. Phone 1-800-555-0159 to order your repair kit.

3. Please greet your family for me.

4. I'm sorry I can't help you, Marsha, but the policy must be enforced.

## APPLYING THE INDIRECT APPROACH TO BAD NEWS MESSAGES

The indirect approach can be applied to all three types of bad news messages: request refusals, adjustment refusals, and unexpected bad news.

# Request Refusals

Customer and employee requests—invitations, orders, credit applications, or correspondence related to policy—are taken very seriously. Also taken seriously are the messages written when these requests must be refused. Because customer and employee satisfaction are important to business success, writers use the indirect approach when refusing requests.

Open a request refusal with a buffer that relates to the receiver and/or the request. Next, give the reason(s) for the refusal. The explanation should focus on the receiver or should be neutral. The reader may recognize that the decision also benefits the writer, but the writer should not stress this point. The bad news, presented after the explanation for it, may be either expressed or implied. A counterproposal and a positive, friendly closing complete the message.

Pam Salijak, an inventory clerk at Winwood Restaurant Supply, has requested a 5 percent salary increase. Pam, a single mother of two, recently purchased an older home that needs repairs. Pam has worked at WRS for five years. Her performance has been consistently rated as outstanding. In fact, in her last annual review, Pam earned higher ratings than anyone else in her department. Her supervisor faces the challenge of keeping Pam's morale high while telling her a raise won't be awarded. Figure 5-1 on page 96 presents one way to respond to Pam's request.

Notice that the buffer is an accurate statement of what has happened but that it does not indicate whether the request is being approved or denied. The explanation describes the company's policy and shows how it benefits the receiver and other employees. The bad news is expressed with the counterproposal and linked to it. The positive, friendly close spins naturally from the counterproposal. In addition, it stresses Pam's record of service, hard work, and loyalty.

> Request refusals follow the indirect approach.

## [THINKING IT THROUGH 5-5]

## Resale

Assume that Pam Salijak did not tell her supervisor why she wanted a raise. Prepare a resale paragraph that could be used in place of the counterproposal.

**MEMORANDUM**

TO:        Pam Salijak

FROM:      Linc Whitlock  *lw*

DATE:      March 23, 200-

SUBJECT:   Salary Increase

[1] Pam, your request for a salary increase has been received and carefully considered.

[2] WRS wants to ensure that each employee receives individual attention and that the time between evaluations is the same for every worker. Therefore, cost-of-living raises are awarded in January, and merit increase reviews are conducted during each employee's anniversary month.

[3] Because you received a 3 percent cost-of-living raise in January and will be reviewed for a merit increase in July, your request to be considered for a salary increase at this time is denied. The Winwood Employee Credit Union (WECU) may, however, be of help to you in meeting your remodeling needs. Home improvement loans are currently being offered at a low 7.6 percent interest rate. In addition, WECU maintains listings of carpenters and craftspeople who do high-quality work at reasonable rates.

[4] Pam, WECU serves all employees who have been with the company for at least six months. A $25 deposit is all that's necessary to establish membership. You've been a hard-working, loyal employee for five years. To learn more about the services offered by the Credit Union, call 555-0134 or stop by Room 225, Building K.

**Annotations**

[1] Buffer

[2] Explanation

[3] Bad News and Counter-proposal

[4] Positive, Friendly Close

**Figure 5-1**
Request Refusal

> *Claims are denied using the indirect approach.*

## Adjustment Refusals

In Chapter 4, you learned that claims are viewed as good news because they give the organization an opportunity to redeem itself, identify and correct problems, and promote goodwill. Unfortunately, not all claims are valid. Some claims reflect consumer negligence, some ask for extraordinary remedies, and some are frivolous or simply false. If a business is to be profitable and maintain its integrity, it must honor valid claims and refuse all others. The indirect approach is used for messages written in response to claims that are denied.

Adjustment refusals begin with a buffer that relates to the topic but not the bad news. Next, the writer presents reasons for the refusal. Facts are more convincing than opinions. If an investigation was conducted or tests were run, say so. The results are the foundation for the bad news.

Receiver viewpoint must be considered when writing the explanation. Therefore, writers often use the passive rather than the active voice.

Active Voice: You dropped the clock.
Passive Voice: The clock has been dropped.

The passive voice can temper negative news.

Give the bad news in implied or expressed terms. Avoid words like *grant* and *allow*. Such words suggest that the writer has power and that the gap in status between sender and receiver is large. If possible, offer a counterproposal; otherwise, include a resale statement. End pleasantly, perhaps by encouraging the reader to act on the counterproposal.

Avoid words that emphasize the writer's power.

Remember, word-of-mouth advertising is very powerful. The manner in which claims are handled affects the way claimants view writers and their organizations. If customers are satisfied with the way a claim is handled, *even when it is refused*, they are apt to speak well of the organization. They will become informal goodwill ambassadors for the organization.

Alyson Chambers has requested that the electric wok she purchased one month ago be repaired without charge. She states, "The first time I used the wok, it worked well. When I went to use it last night, however, the wok wouldn't heat. I don't understand why. All I did was use it, clean it, and put it away." Your technician inspected the heating element and quickly discovered the problem. The element had gotten wet—something the owner's manual warns against. Figure 5-2 presents a bad news response to the claim.

Notice that the adjustment refusal in Figure 5-2 introduces the topic in the subject line. Doing so allows the writer to develop the buffer around the idea that the heating element is vital to successful wok cookery. The explanation section presents the findings in a nonaccusatory manner and states clearly that the warranty is no longer in effect. The counterproposal offers the reader two options, and the closing makes action easy. The statement about wok cooking being healthy cooking links the closing paragraph to the opening paragraph and enhances the overall unity of the message.

A subject line can be useful in introducing the topic of a message.

One final comment about refusal messages: Be sure they are timely. Delays in responding to requests or claims could make readers angry and less willing to accept bad news.

Refusals must be timely.

When Debbi Fields tried to get capital to start a cookie store, one potential funder told her, "A cookie store is a bad idea. Besides, the market research reports say America likes crispy cookies, not soft and chewy cookies like you make." The person who bluntly conveyed this bad news to Mrs. Fields missed a tremendous investment opportunity.

**Major Electric Company**

1611 Akron Peninsula Road  Akron, OH 44313-7929

July 17, 200-

Ms. Alyson Chambers
168 Summer Point
Edwardsville, IL 62025-5723

Dear Ms. Chambers

**WOK HEATING ELEMENT**

| 1 | Wok cooking offers health-conscious people delicious meals with very low fat content. This is possible because the heat is spread evenly throughout the cooking surface. The key to even cooking temperatures is the heating element.

| 2 | When your letter and package arrived, they were delivered to our repair division. Upon opening the element's casing, the technician discovered that the parts inside were wet—a clear sign that the element had been placed in water or that water had been spilled on it. The owner's manual for the wok

| 3 | indicates that the heating element should be cleaned by wiping it with a damp cloth. Exposing the element to water would cause the unit to fail. The warranty would be void.

| 4 | To restore your wok to working condition, the heating element must be replaced. New elements are available for $29.95; reconditioned elements are available for $19.95. A new element would have the same one-year warranty as the original element. The warranty on reconditioned units is in effect for just three months.

| 5 | To order either a new or a reconditioned element, phone 1-800-555-0190. Within ten days after placing your order, you'll again be "woking" your way to good health.

Sincerely yours

*Vicki Haugen*

Vicki Haugen
Customer Service Representative

**Annotations**

1 Buffer

2 Explanation

3 Bad News

4 Counterproposal

5 Positive, Action Close

**Figure 5-2**
Adjustment Refusal

According to *Rotten Rejections*, by Andre Bernard, a publisher rejected Ernest Hemingway's book *The Torrents of Spring* with this letter: "It would be in extremely rotten taste, to say nothing of being horribly cruel, should we want to publish it." About his novel *Carrie*, Stephen King's editor wrote: "We are not interested in science fiction which deals with negative utopias." And when Oscar Wilde sent his publisher *Lady Windermere's Fan*, the response was: "My dear sir, I have read your manuscript. Oh, my dear sir!"

## Subject Lines

Assume you are the claimant in the situation leading to Figure 5-2. Would you have a positive, negative, or neutral reaction to a message that began with each of the following subject lines? Why?

1. DEFECTIVE HEATING ELEMENT

2. WET HEATING ELEMENT

3. YOUR REQUEST FOR REPAIR

4. REPLACEMENT OF HEATING ELEMENT

5. REPAIR COSTS

## Unexpected Bad News

This type of bad news message deserves special attention. More than any other type of bad news, unexpected bad news will be received with disappointment or anger. The reason is simple—readers aren't expecting any message, let alone bad news. Layoffs, terminations, reductions in benefits, increases in price, and reductions in service are all unexpected bad news.

Unexpected bad news messages, like other bad news messages, begin with a buffer. Because the receiver isn't aware of the topic of the message, the buffer must outline it clearly. The buffer in unexpected bad news messages may, therefore, be longer than the buffer in request refusal or adjustment refusal messages.

> Receiver analysis is especially important in unexpected bad news situations.

After providing a clear, complete explanation of the situation, the writer gives the bad news. While implied bad news is less emphatic, expressed bad news may be needed for clarity.

Counterproposals show a writer's empathy for a receiver's situation.

The counterproposal/resale section of an unexpected bad news message is critical. Any alternative solution or offer of assistance will show interest in readers and help them to accept the bad news. The message should close with a positive, optimistic statement.

Josh Peltier is the director of a nature center. He must notify its patrons (schools, youth groups, senior citizen groups, etc.) that the center's offerings will change due to budget constraints. Figure 5-3 shows how Josh approached this unexpected bad news situation.

The brief, positive buffer stresses the mission of the center and its value to the public. The mission and value theme is continued in the explanation paragraph. Positive wording and a focus on what will be done minimize the bad news. Resale begins in the last sentence of paragraph 2 and continues into the final paragraph. Message unity is achieved by closing the message as it was opened, with a statement about the public value of the facility.

The address and salutation are missing because this form letter will be merged with information maintained in the Center's patron database.

## THE DIRECT APPROACH

Occasionally, bad news should be conveyed directly.

Rules, it has been said, are meant to be broken, and that is the case with the approach to writing bad news messages. Although an indirect approach is used in *almost* all cases involving bad news, a direct or modified direct approach may be best in special cases.

The direct approach to bad news messages presents the bad news in the opening paragraph and then explains the reason for it. Resale is included, if appropriate, and the message ends with a positive or neutral close.

Use the direct approach if previous experience with a receiver suggests that the indirect approach will be unsuccessful. Also use the direct approach when engaged in labor-management negotiations or when recalling a product. In the first situation, the indirect approach could be viewed as being deceptive; in the second, customer safety dictates that the main idea be foremost in the message.

Use the modified direct approach when confirming information that has already been presented orally.

The modified direct approach omits the buffer and begins with the explanation. Except for this, the message follows the indirect bad news pattern. Use the modified direct approach when confirming or documenting negative news previously conveyed orally. This oral/written communication blend works well when the bad news has considerable emotional impact. For example, a supervisor who must fire an employee would initially convey the news in a one-to-one meeting and then follow up with a written confirmation. Similarly, if a company had a

**WOODVILLE NATURE CENTER**
750 Cameron Woods Drive • Angola, IN: 46703-8816
(260) 555-0133 • http://www.wnc.org

Current Date

<<AddressBlock>>

<<GreetingLine>>

1 The Woodville Nature Center has been a valuable learning and recreation resource for nearly a quarter century. Every year, the Center hosts thousands of visitors; each leaves with a greater appreciation for our environment and the plants and animals with which we share it.

2 At its May meeting, the WNC Advisory Council unanimously reaffirmed the Center's educational and recreational mission and approved the annual budget. Despite stagnant endowment interest rates, reduced foundation funding, and inflation, the Council has decided to retain all of

3 WNC's programs for the coming year. To achieve this goal, councilors agreed to limit hours of operation and to reduce the frequency of guided tours. Effective July 1, WNC will be open from 11 a.m. to 7 p.m. Monday

4 through Saturday and from noon to 5 p.m. Sunday. Guided tours will be available on Tuesday, Thursday, Saturday, and Sunday. Self-guided tours will continue to be available seven days a week.

5 All Center programs are detailed on the Web at http://www.wnc.org. As an added convenience, material orders and tour requests may be made online. We urge you to make plans now for summer and fall visits to Woodville—the finest nature center in the tri-state region.

Sincerely

*Josh Peltier*

Josh Peltier
Director

Annotations

1 Buffer

2 Explanation

3 Bad News

4 Resale

5 Positive Close

**Figure 5-3**
Unexpected Bad News Message

longstanding relationship with one supplier and then decided to award a contract to another, the news would probably be conveyed face-to-face or by telephone first. This technique shows personal and organizational sensitivity.

# PROPER USE OF TECHNOLOGY

Technology has had a tremendous effect on the way written communication is created and transmitted. When it comes to bad news messages, though, writers should carefully consider the role technology can and should play.

Clearly, e-mail represents an efficient way to the original respond to questions or complaints. If the original messages were sent by e-mail, it is appropriate to respond to them electronically, using the indirect or direct approach as dictated by receiver and situation analysis. Before sending bad news by e-mail, read the message several times to ensure that the style, accuracy, and tone are appropriate.

When the bad news has substantial emotional impact, traditional Distribution methods should be used. E-mail is too informal.

## CHAPTER SUMMARY

- Bad news business messages include request refusals, adjustment refusals, and unexpected bad news.
- The indirect approach is typically used when conveying bad news.
- A bad news message organized by the indirect approach has five sections:

  1. *Buffer.* An opening related to the topic of the message but not related to the bad news.
  2. *Explanation.* Convincing reasons intended to lead the reader to accept the negative news.
  3. *Bad News.* An implied or expressed statement given minimal emphasis in the message.
  4. *Counterproposal/Resale.* Alternative solutions (counterproposal) or comments (resale) designed to restore, maintain, or build goodwill between the sender and the receiver. If neither a counterproposal nor resale material is possible, this section presents additional reasons for the decision.
  5. *Closing.* A positive, friendly, sometimes action-oriented statement that relates to the topic without referencing the bad news.

- The direct approach may be used in special circumstances, as dictated by receiver and situation analysis.

  - The direct approach presents the bad news in the opening paragraph.
  - The modified direct approach omits the buffer and begins with the explanation.

- E-mail can be used to deliver some bad news messages, but bad news that is sensitive should be sent by letter or conveyed orally.

*Chapter 5: Writing Bad News Messages*

## Section I: Work-Related Messages

The following exercises require you to apply the indirect or direct approach in writing work-related messages. Read the directions carefully. Unless your instructor tells you otherwise, use the style you prefer for memos or letters (several styles are presented in Appendix A). Begin letters with the date (no return address is needed). Send e-mails to your instructor. Use today's date unless another date is given, and invent reasonable details as necessary. Apply the 4Cs of communication that you learned about in Chapter 3, and remember to proofread your messages for mechanics.

### Request Refusals

1.  You have been invited to join the local chapter of Alpha Beta Gamma (ABG), an active group for business professionals. Each chapter of the group has a membership limit of 25; the last time the local chapter accepted a member was in 2002. According to the invitation, signed by Membership Chair E. Jacob Zenk, the initiation ceremony—which new members *must* attend—is scheduled for February 20. As sales manager for Falls Industries, you travel frequently. In fact, you will be out of town February 19–22, meeting with an important client.

    Assume that you have decided to decline the invitation to join Alpha Beta Gamma.

    a.  Who will read your message?

    b.  Will you use a letter, memo, or other format (specify)?

    c.  What idea will you use in the buffer?

    d.  What details will you furnish as part of your explanation?

    e.  Will you imply or express the bad news?

    f.  Will you use a counterproposal, provide resale information, or offer additional reasons?

    g.  What will be the basis of your counterproposal/resale/reason section?

*continued on next page*

h. What positive item can you use as a closing?

i. Are enclosures needed? If so, what?

j. Using the notes you made in items a–i above, write the message.

2. Refer to Application 1. Assume the role of president of the St. Louis chapter of Alpha Beta Gamma. J. P. Riche, a prospective member, has asked that initiation ceremony requirements be modified to allow her to join ABG at the March 20 meeting rather than on February 20. Much as you wish you could accommodate her request, you can't. The requirement is set by the national board, not the local board. Prepare a message that refuses the request. Use the date of January 4. Ms. Riche's address is 1304 Geyer Court, Kirkwood, MO 63122-7100.

3. You work for Will Macor, manager of the Accounting Department at Billings Manufacturing. Your company pays tuition and fees for employees who take classes related to their jobs. When workers want to enroll in a class, they submit a written request to their supervisor. After completing an approved class, workers submit their grade report and proof of expenses for reimbursement.

Today (August 23) is the first day of Will's five-week vacation. Although Will won't be in today, he has left some work for you to complete. Among the items he's left for you are the following memo and draft response. Will's note says, "Finish this refusal for me; sign my name." Do as Will asks.

*continued on next page*

*Chapter 5: Writing Bad News Messages*

*Incoming Memo:*

**TO:**       Will Macor, Manager

**FROM:**     Pamela Fox, Account Clerk  *PF*

**DATE:**     August 20, 200-

**SUBJECT:**  Course Enrollment

Will, may I have your permission to enroll in the following class at Cambridge Community College?

COMM 101 Mass Media

Mass media is a topic that's always interested me, and I'd like to learn more about it in this three-credit class. Fall term begins September 11; I'll need your approval by September 4 to register.

---

*Draft Memo:*

**TO:**       Pamela Fox, Account Clerk

**FROM:**     Will Macor, Manager

**DATE:**     August 23, 200-

**SUBJECT:**

Pam, it's good to see that you're interested in taking classes at Cambridge Community Col-lege. CCC is a fine school with many classes that can benefit Billings' employees.

In order to promote professional growth and ensure that workers are aware of innovations in their fields, Billings pays tuition and fees for workers who enroll in courses directly related to their work.

---

4. You are the program coordinator for a new company called Mardian Professional Development (MPD). Mardian hires well-known authors and speakers to conduct seminars on topics of interest to business professionals. To meet expenses and to have the critical mass necessary to engage participants in small- and large-group activities, you must enroll 10 people in each seminar. The maximum number of participants is 25. Seminar leaders appreciate the small class size, and smaller numbers make it easy for you to locate sites for the sessions.

Brochures are prepared and distributed throughout the nation. Each brochure describes a particular seminar and its dates and locations. The brochure includes a registration form. Only mail registrations are accepted because the full fee must be submitted with the form. One seminar currently being offered by MPD is "Improving Your Written Communication Skills." Cities, sites, dates, and current enrollments for the seminar are as follows:

*continued on next page* ▼

| City | Site | Date | Enrollment |
|------|------|------|-----------|
| Albuquerque, New Mexico | Old Town Center | May 27 | 7 |
| Chicago, Illinois | Executive Hotel | May 23 | 21 |
| Dallas, Texas | Houston House | June 2 | 25 |
| Fort Worth, Texas | Rio Grande Suites | June 3 | 18 |
| St. Louis, Missouri | Arch Plaza | May 24 | 20 |

Today is May 17, the closing date for enrollment in the writing seminar. You received three reservations for the Dallas seminar, which was filled as of May 10.

a. Prepare a form letter to be sent to the people who registered for the Albuquerque seminar telling them it has been canceled.

b. Prepare a form letter to be sent to the three people whose registrations were received after the Dallas seminar was filled. Pay special attention to the counterproposal section; use it to persuade the readers to attend the seminar in Fort Worth. Give them a deadline of May 24 to respond.

5. Assume you are the owner of three movie rental stores. About six months ago, a national movie rental chain opened a store in your community. Last week, a national advertisement for the chain announced that it would no longer charge a fee if materials were returned up to three days late. One of your customers left a letter for you at one of the stores asking you to do the same.

   You know the other store's promotion will have a negative impact on your stores, but you believe the problem will be short-lived. You have generous rental periods, and your fees for late return are low. Only 6 percent of your customer base has paid a late fee during the past year. You take pride in the selection of movies you offer and keep wait lists for high-demand DVDs and videos. You've been known to shift inventory from one store to another to ensure that customers aren't kept on the wait list for more than a few days. Write to the customer denying his request (Tim Dahl, 159 Ridgewood Road, Baltimore, MD 21210-2536).

6. Helena O'Brien teaches pilates. She's written to your company, Sims Publications, requesting 250 reprints of "A Healthier You." She wants to give the reprints to people who enroll in her classes. The article appeared on pages 113–118 of the June 2004 issue of Exercise. Rather than send so many copies of the article to one person, you will send her one copy and give her permission to reprint as many copies as she needs for her students. Your message should include the reprint statement you want to appear on the copies. (Hint: Check a reference manual for ideas on how to write the credit line.)

7. Employees of your company may participate in any of four different health plans. Employees are free to move from one plan to another as their needs change, but shifts between plans may occur only once each calendar year. This rule, which is common among insurance providers, keeps processing costs low. Today (August 17) you, the employee benefits clerk, receive a request from Virginia Marthaller to change from Plan A to Plan B. A check of Ms. Marthaller's file reveals that she switched to Plan A on June 15. Prepare an appropriate message to this auditing department worker.

8. You manage the business office at a large mall. Twice each year for the past six years, you have hosted an unpaid marketing intern from Logan University. The internship director with whom you worked has retired, and his replacement, Bob Zachary, has written asking whether you will

*continued on next page*

*Chapter 5: Writing Bad News Messages*

participate in the program again this year. Among the changes Mr. Zachary has instituted is the requirement that interns be paid. You've decided not to participate in the program under the new terms—you firmly believe that an internship is a learning experience and that interns are not with the mall long enough to contribute to its productivity. Convey your decision to Mr. Zachary at Logan University, 100 Bisbee Road, Bisbee, AZ 85603-1121.

9. As the new communications director for a paper products company, you often receive requests to donate products (e.g., facial tissue or bath tissue) to charitable organizations. Your organization has a philosophy that endorses corporate giving to agencies that operate in the communities where you have offices and factories. Prepare a form letter that could be sent to organizations that do not meet your giving criteria.

10. When you checked your e-mail this morning, you found a message from your supervisor, Adele Price, asking whether you could finish a staffing report a week earlier than the original due date because she will be out of town on business and would like to review the report while away. Normally, you organize your projects to enable you to complete them with days to spare. This time, though, your schedule has no flexibility. Your assistant resigned, the database you needed had to be updated before you could use it, and you will be taking at least three days of sick leave next week because of minor surgery that was scheduled months ago. Prepare an appropriate response.

11. As manager of TV station YNWS, you frequently receive requests for studio tours. You welcome the opportunity to host guests and explain television production to them, but you restrict tours to non-show times. Today, you received a request from Chuck Zeagle, who owns Daytime Smiles Child Care Center. Chuck has asked for permission to have 12 children (ages 3 to 5) visit your studio during the broadcast of your noon news and entertainment show. Refuse Chuck's request. YNWS is located at 150 Market Street, Philadelphia, PA 19106-3015.

12. J. J. Venk of Venk Properties has written seeking a character reference for Paul Hudel, one of the employees in your fast-food restaurant franchise. Apparently, Paul and two of his friends want to rent a house from Mr. Venk. Your policy is to maintain a professional relationship with your employees and to treat their employment records as confidential. Unless the employee signs a release giving you permission to respond and listing the specific person or business to which you are free to comment, you will provide only the dates of the individual's employment (e.g., May 2003 to present). Although you see Paul regularly, he hasn't spoken with you about his housing plans or authorized you to be a reference on his behalf. Respond to Mr. Venk's request.

## Adjustment Refusals

13. You own a cosmetology school. As part of their training, students work in an on-site salon under the supervision of licensed instructors. Yesterday, you received an angry letter from Ginny Twinz. She says that one of your students wrecked her mother's silk blouse by careless use of the sprayer while washing her hair during her regular appointment last week. She's asked for $60 to replace the garment and for three months' free styling services for her mother, Virgene Crawford.

You've spoken with the stylist and her supervisor. Both indicate that Mrs. Crawford sneezed several times while the student was washing her hair. The body movement and Mrs. Crawford's reaching for a tissue caused some water to get on the sleeve of her blouse. The student immediately apologized and informed her supervisor of the incident. The supervisor spoke with Mrs. Crawford and offered to have the blouse cleaned. Mrs. Crawford refused, saying the blouse was

*continued on next page*

old and in need of routine cleaning. When she left, she praised the student and left her a generous tip. Deny the claim. Ms. Twinz's address is 119 N. Baldwin Street, Madison, WI 53703-3014.

14. You manage an advertising business that provides custom-made novelty products. Last month, the Gurion Company ordered 1,500 insulated mugs from you. Each mug was to show the company name, logo, and motto. Today, you received a fax from Petri Gurion, a vice president at the company. He's irate because the mugs say "The Gorian Company." He wants you to replace the mugs, deliver them at your expense, and refund 50 percent of the purchase price. You try to avoid content errors by sending customers a proof (draft illustration) before production begins. You've examined your records and have found that this text, including the error, was approved by someone with the initials *plg*. Deny the claim. The Gurion Company's address is 1140 W. Broward Boulevard, Ft. Lauderdale, FL 33312-1639.

15. The gallery you manage sells a variety of artwork, including framed and unframed paintings and prints. The walls of your shop are adorned with attractively framed items. Each has a small card posted on or near it showing the title of the work, the name of the artist, and the "framed" and "unframed" price. Last week, Kwan Chee purchased a framed print of Arden Harvey's *Raging River* as a gift for a colleague who was retiring. Mr. Chee was in a hurry the day he made the selection. After removing it from the wall and setting it on the counter, he asked you to bill him and said someone would stop for the package two days later. Everything seemed to go as planned until today, two weeks after Mr. Chee visit to your shop. In the mail you find a letter from a very angry Mr. Chee, who insists you overcharged him. Although he makes reference to the framed print, he quotes the price of the unframed work. Handle his claim. Mr. Chee's address is 3147 North Quainton Court, Fayetteville, AR 72703-4541.

16. You work for Marzetti Landscaping. Last fall, you planted five fruit trees in Emma Carol's yard. At the time Ms. Carol purchased the trees and again when they were planted, you stressed the importance of keeping the trees well watered. Ms. Carol told you her work required her to travel often, but that she would do her best. It's now April, and Ms. Carol has asked you to replace three of the trees because they did not survive the winter. You went to her home while she was away on business and examined the trees. Three were dead, and the other two were desperately in need of water. Based on what you saw during your investigation, deny Ms. Carol's claim. Her address is 14 Main Street, Stockbridge, MA 01262-9701.

17. Marlow Gunderson has written to you expressing dissatisfaction with your company's salsa. The product, he asserts, is "hotter than the desert sun in August." He doesn't think that the symbol you use to indicate the warmth of the salsa (red flames; 1 = mild; 5 = extreme) is effective. He goes on to suggest a new symbol and wording that, frankly, isn't appropriate for a label; he's enclosed a bill for $300, which he says represents the cost of his services. Respond to his claim. Mr. Gunderson's address is P.O. Box 250, Vaughn, NM 88353-0550.

18. You work as a customer service agent for a regional airline. Louis Rodrigo has requested a $140 refund on the unused portion of a round-trip ticket, which he enclosed with his letter. He says he arrived at the airport 30 minutes before the flight. After making his way to the front of a long line, he learned the departure time had been changed and he had missed his flight. There were no other flights that day, so he spent the night at a hotel and returned on another airline. He's asking for $400 to cover the cost of his new ticket and overnight stay.

*continued on next page*

Mr. Rodrigo's original ticket was purchased during a promotion that offered travelers a low price in return for 30-day advance booking and a minimum five-day stay that included a Saturday night. All ads and the ticket receipt clearly indicated "No Refunds." Mr. Rodrigo is correct in saying that the flight time was changed; however, new itineraries were mailed to those affected by the change. Every itinerary also bears a bright orange sticker saying, "To ensure adequate time for check-in and boarding, please arrive at the airport at least 60 minutes before the scheduled departure time." Respond to the claim. Mr. Rodrigo's address is 421 Panorama Drive, Bakersfield, CA 93305-1024.

19. You are the treasurer of the Young Professionals Network, a local group that meets from noon to 1:30 p.m. the second Tuesday of each month. The luncheon meeting typically includes 30 minutes to socialize, 30 minutes for lunch, and a 30-minute program. Attendees choose between two meals; reservations must be submitted by noon the Friday before the meeting. You place the food order with the restaurant. Members pay you the day of the event; you pay the restaurant. Because people were making reservations and then not attending the meeting, which left YPN to pay for the uneaten meals, the executive board decided several months ago to bill those who didn't honor their reservations. Notice of this new policy was included in the last two monthly newsletters. You sent your bills three business days ago and today received an e-mail from Steve Coach objecting to being charged for a meal he didn't eat. He notes that this is the first meeting he's missed and that because "things come up in business," the group should be more flexible. Deny Steve's request to waive the meal charge.

20. You are a travel agent who specializes in organizing spring break tours to Mexico. Students make an initial $150 deposit and then pay the remainder of the cost, which varies by date and destination, in three equal installments. You will refund half the deposit if students cancel within two weeks of their initial sign-up; otherwise, neither the deposit nor payments are refundable. Your brochures and contract clearly outline these financial arrangements. You have just received a request from Tanisha France saying that, for personal reasons, she will be unable to participate in your tour to Acapulco and asking that you refund her payments to date ($530). Deny her request. Ms. France's address is 1804 Halstad Drive, Stevens Point, WI 54481-8583.

## Unexpected Bad News

21. You manage a fitness center that pays a $15 bonus to employees for each new member they enroll. During the enrollment process, staff are to complete several forms, collect fees, and enter data into the computer. During the past three weeks, you've noticed that Damian Jurek has omitted some of the paperwork and has not entered complete information into the computer. As a result, members and other staff have been inconvenienced. You have spoken with Damian and have told him he will no longer receive $15 per new member if he fails to complete all enrollment tasks. Rather, you will award him $5; the remaining $10 will go to whoever completes the enrollment process. Prepare a memo that confirms the arrangement while encouraging Damian to do better.

22. You are a programmer for a travel agency specializing in overseas tours. One of the tours your firm is currently offering is a seven-day trip to London, England. Included in the $2,150 package are airfare, hotel accommodations, breakfast each day, a bus tour of the city, two theater performances, and a day trip to Windsor Castle. A $500 nonrefundable deposit is required when reservations are made. Your clients pay you in U.S. dollars, but you must pay your London expenses in British currency, called pounds. The value of the U.S. dollar against the British pound changes

*continued on next page* ▼

daily. Unfortunately, the value of the dollar has fallen over the past few months. In fact, to cover expenses, the price of the package must be increased to $2,475. The people who signed up for the tour knew that the $2,150 rate was subject to change, but you aren't sure how they will react to a $325 increase. Your task is to tell them.

23. The bank at which you work offers many services to its clients, including safety deposit boxes. The boxes are available in four sizes. Bank patrons lease their boxes on a year-to-year basis. An annual fee is charged; bills are sent one month before the leases expire. Due to security improvement costs and increased access hours, the bank has decided to raise the box fee. The sizes, current fees, and new fees are as follows:

| Sizes | Current Fees | New Fees |
|---|---|---|
| 2" × 5" box | $10.00 | $12.50 |
| 4" × 6" box | $12.50 | $15.00 |
| 6" × 10" box | $18.00 | $22.00 |
| 8" × 12" box | $25.00 | $30.00 |

Prepare a form message that can be sent to each person whose lease is about to expire notifying him or her about the rate increase.

24. For the past month, the employees of your firm have donated money to help Bobby Burns. Bobby, the eight-month-old son of maintenance worker Harry Burns, needed a kidney transplant. Containers were placed in several locations throughout the building; people were encouraged to make cash deposits. The drive was very successful; $1,873 has been donated. This morning you learn that Bobby died yesterday. Prepare a memo to the staff telling them the bad news. Be sure to indicate what will be done with the money that has been collected.

25. You work for a government agency that was recently embarrassed by a news story that reported one of your department heads racked up $1,147 in cell phone charges in August and $1,733 in September. The calls could be justified, but enrollment in a plan that led to those charges could not. The problem has been corrected, but the incident has led to the development of a new cell phone policy. As administrative director, your task is to announce the policy to employees in your agency. The following key details should be part of the message; additional information can be found on the agency's website. Personal calls are OK in an emergency, but they must be noted on the monthly bill submitted for reimbursement. Violators will be charged 15 cents a minute, with a penalty of an additional 10 cents a minute. Employees who travel on government business may incur up to $5 per day in charges for personal calls; for call totals in excess of $5, the above-mentioned charges and penalties will apply.

26. You are a sales associate with Briarley Furniture. Three months ago, you worked with Sheila and Roberto Alm to select living room and dining room furniture for their new home. The Alms were delighted when their dining room furniture arrived a week ahead of the projected delivery date. The news you have for them today, however, won't please them. The company that manufactures the sofa, love seat, and chairs the Alms ordered just notified you that the fabric they chose is out of stock. The Alms have two options: (1) They may wait for the fabric of their choice; their furniture will be delivered in 10–12 weeks. (2) They may select an in-stock fabric; their furniture will be delivered in 4–6 weeks. Write to your customers. The Alms' address is 293 Walnut Street, Grafton, WV 26354-1643.

*Chapter 5: Writing Bad News Messages*

27. For the past eight years, Kurtz Paper Company has sponsored a picnic for its workers and their families or guests. The all-day event is held at a local park. Food and beverages are provided. There are games for adults and children; prizes are awarded. The past year has been a difficult one for Kurtz. A fire severely damaged one of the warehouses. Customers went elsewhere for their products; revenues fell. Also, the actual cost of installing a new pollution control system far exceeded the estimate. Therefore, this year's company picnic will be replaced with an "employees only" ice cream social. Notify employees of the change.

28. As business manager for Golden Glow Senior Residence, you face the task of telling residents that the cost of relocating from one apartment to another will rise from $40 to $400. Each time an apartment becomes vacant, it is thoroughly cleaned. The new rate more nearly matches the actual cost of this process in terms of time and materials. Your residents, most of whom are on fixed incomes, won't like this news. Senior citizen housing is in short supply. Because your facility has offered vacant units to tenants before applicants, many people moved into their current apartments with the intent of moving to apartments with more space or a better view. Prepare a form message. The address of Golden Glow Senior Residence is 32245 Old Nash Road, Seward, AK 99664-9703.

29. You are the director of the Greater Prospect Solid Waste Treatment Center. Garbage haulers collect waste from homes and businesses and bring it to your center for inspection before it is repacked and trucked to landfills. At several recent meetings, your department heads have commented that the number of unacceptable items they have found during inspections has increased dramatically. You have agreed to prepare a message to be included with trash collection bills sent during the next three months (experience has taught you that one mailing isn't sufficient). Some items are deemed unacceptable because they contain toxic materials (e.g., lead or mercury), could be recycled (e.g., metals, plastics, and paper), or both (appliances). Specifically, you must tell your customers not to put the following items in the trash:

- Recyclable materials      Household hazardous waste (certain paints, stains, cleaning products, and pesticides; motor oil; car batteries; etc.)
- Tires      Electronic waste (computers, copiers, fax machines, etc.)
- Yard waste      Major appliances (microwaves, freezers, water heaters, air conditioners, etc.)
- Asbestos      Medical sharps (needles and other sharp objects)

The need to be conscientious about keeping unacceptable items out of the trash won't come as good news to your receivers. Their first question is apt to be, *How do I get rid of these things?* So, be sure to give them the location of your Household Hazardous Waste facility (10 River Road, Prospect, MD 21613-0202) and the hours, too.

30. You work in the administrative services department for the City of Smithville. One of your tasks is scheduling use of city vehicles. During the past month you have received calls and letters from citizens of Smithville complaining that they have seen city cars parked at local grocery stores, malls, and entertainment facilities. Prepare a memo reminding workers that city cars are to be used only for city business.

31. Deborah Winston, your supervisor and manager of the accounting department, has asked you to prepare a memo telling workers that receipts will now be required for reimbursement of all business-related expenses. Currently, only expenses in excess of $50 require receipts.

# Section II: Personal-Business Messages

The following exercises relate to using the indirect approach in writing situations you might face in your personal life. Read the directions carefully. Use the personal-business letter format (refer to Appendix A). Use today's date, and invent reasonable details as necessary. Apply the 4Cs of good communication presented in Chapter 3. Plan before you write, and proofread for mechanics.

32. You volunteer at a local homeless shelter and soup kitchen on weekends. You enjoy working with the shelter's clients, but because you have considerable experience with computers, the coordinator has asked you to devote the majority of your volunteer hours to the business side of the operation. When you got to the office today, you found a note from the coordinator asking you to install two software programs. You quickly noticed that the programs are not licensed. Although you know the shelter has a small operating budget, you object to installing pirated software. Convey the bad news to Olivia Newfeld.

33. You have been invited to serve on the planning committee for your high school reunion but have decided to decline. Write to your classmate, Barb Zelnick, telling her the bad news. Barb's address is 1849 Terrace Drive, Minot, ND 58703-1134.

34. You belong to the student chapter of a professional organization The local group that sponsors your chapter selected you to be this year's recipient of its "Rising Star" award. You were the organization's guest at its dinner meeting last night, at which time you received a plaque and a $100 check. Your name is spelled correctly on the check, but not on the plaque. You didn't want to destroy the mood or embarrass anyone at the dinner, so you decided to wait until today to write to Jason Kilpatrick, the president, to tell him the bad news. Jason's address is 506 Brentwood Road, Marshalltown, IA 50158-3726.

35. You have been asked by the president of your school to serve as its representative to the local United Way's planning committee. This is quite an honor and something that would look good on your résumé. Also, you believe in contributing not only money but also time to charitable organizations. If you accept the responsibility, you would be expected to attend biweekly meetings—some at midday, others in the evening—throughout July and August; participate in the kickoff barbeque; and coordinate all fundraising efforts at your school. Write a message declining the invitation.

36. Your good friend Terry Brennan attends school in another city. While Terry was home for a break several months ago, you and she had lunch. You chatted about lots of things, including your mutual love of books. During the conversation, Terry mentioned a mystery novel she'd just finished and thought you would enjoy. After she returned to school, she mailed it to you. The book was so good you read it from cover to cover and then passed it along to your cousin, Marv. Today you received an e-mail from Terry asking you to mail the book to her because she wants to give it back to the person from whom she had borrowed it. This is the first you knew that the book wasn't Terry's or that you weren't free to share it with someone else. Unfortunately, Marv can't find the book. Respond to Terry's request.

37. You have been invited to join Beta Sigma Rho, a national honor society that has a chapter on your campus. The local group meets monthly and engages in a variety of educational and service activities. The national group publishes a quarterly journal and sponsors an online forum where members can discuss items of interest. The initiation fee is $50, national dues are $25 annually, and local dues are $20 a term. You would like to join, but time and money are a problem. Decline the invitation.

# Writing Persuasive Messages

A hypnotist slowly waves a watch or other object before a subject's eyes and says, "You are getting sleepy, very sleepy." Once the subject is relaxed, the hypnotist gets him or her to do things that ordinarily would not be acceptable: walk like a duck, moo like a cow, tango without a partner, or laugh when a particular word is spoken. The techniques used in business messages are far less dramatic, but the desired result is the same. The sender wants to persuade the receiver to do something he or she may not want to do.

## THE INDIRECT APPROACH

Persuasion is a little bit science, a little bit art. The science stems from techniques that have been developed through experience and experimentation. The art relates to the ability of people to use the techniques effectively.

Persuasion is most often associated with sales messages, but it is employed in other types of business messages as well. Requests, claims, collection messages, and proposals all require persuasion. In fact, anytime someone wants cooperation, money, information, support, or time from someone who is likely to resist, persuasion is required.

If persuaders were allowed to choose, most would prefer to deliver their messages orally, face-to-face. In this setting, the persuader can gauge the receiver's reaction and adjust the message based on what is heard or observed. In addition, an in-person request is harder to refuse than a written one or one delivered by telephone. Time, distance, and cost make it impractical or impossible for all persuasive messages to be delivered in person, so communicators must write persuasive messages. Written messages are more persuasive when they use the indirect approach.

The indirect approach to persuasive messages uses the AIDA plan (*attention*, *interest*, *desire*, and *action*). The parts are presented in sequence, but the result doesn't have to be a four-paragraph message. The topic, reader, and situation will influence the length of the interest and desire sections.

## LEARNING OBJECTIVES

- Learn to write persuasive messages using the indirect approach.
- Use *attention*, *interest*, *desire*, and *action* (AIDA) to make the indirect approach work.
- Write persuasive sales messages, requests, claims, and collection messages.
- Compose effective business proposals.

*Use the indirect approach for persuasive messages.*

*Persuasive messages use the AIDA plan.*

Get your readers' attention in the opening.

# Attention

A persuasive message begins with an attention-getting opening. The opening should involve readers by being of interest to them. Some attention-getting message openers are as follows:

| | |
|---|---|
| *Question*: | Would you like to retire at age 40? |
| *Statement*: | Just 30 minutes of your time could save a life. |
| *Compliment*: | Your generous contribution to Youth Express helped provide summer programs for nearly 300 teenagers. |
| *Bargain/Gift*: | Enjoy the convenience of a cellular phone without roaming charges. |
| *Fact*: | ABC's energy costs have risen 15 percent in the past year. |
| *Problem*: | Handly's market share has fallen to 17 percent. |
| *Story*: | It wasn't easy for Martha after Allen died. By working two jobs, she was able to earn enough money to provide her three young children with simple, nutritious meals and a clean place to live. |

# Interest

Readers will be thinking "What's in it for me?" Your message must answer that question.

After getting the receiver's attention, build interest by keeping the reader focused on the topic. Show how the reader will benefit from the product, service, or idea. Stress the feature or concept that you believe will have the greatest influence on the receiver. One or more of the following appeals usually work:

| | |
|---|---|
| Approval | Love |
| Beauty | Money |
| Comfort | Prestige |
| Convenience | Pride |
| Efficiency | Recognition |
| Enjoyment | Respect |
| Fame | Safety |
| Friendship | Security |
| Good Health | Success |
| Intelligence | Time |
| Justice | Wealth |

66 *The real persuaders are our appetites, our fears and above all our vanity. The skillful propagandist stirs and coaches these internal persuaders.* 99

**-Eric Hoffer**

After generating interest in the topic, the writer works to make the receiver *want* the benefits that have been described—the writer creates desire.

## Attention and Interest

1. For each product, service, or idea in the following list, identify at least two appeals that could be used to show reader benefit. Consider appeals in addition to those listed earlier in this section.

| Idea, Product, or Service | Reader | Appeals |
|---|---|---|
| a. life insurance | new parent | |
| b. changing location of supply cabinet | office supervisor | |
| c. magazine subscription | senior citizen | |
| d. ergonomic chair | office worker | |
| e. tax preparation | sales associate | |

2. Select one of the items above, and write an attention-getting opening for the message.

## Desire

As the writer moves from interest to desire, the focus of the message shifts from an emotional appeal to a logical one. The shift should be so smooth and natural that it is difficult to tell where the interest section ends and the desire section begins. Facts, figures, guarantees, samples, and testimonials can be used to build the receiver's desire to act.

In order to keep the desire section to a reasonable length, writers of-ten include brochures, reports, or other descriptive items with their messages. Savvy writers recognize that such enclosures enhance the desire section but do not replace it. They refer to the enclosures only after developing one or more strong selling points.

In addition to documenting the value of the product, service, or idea, the writer uses the desire section to overcome reader objections. One of the most common objections readers have is cost. Price can't be over-looked, but it can be minimized. Expressing the total cost of a product or service in daily, weekly, or monthly charges can make the price seem affordable. Rather than saying a new air conditioner will cost $750, tell

> Build desire by providing evidence and overcoming objections.

> De-emphasize price.

the reader that cool comfort is available for less than $2.25 a day. Indicate how long it will take for the product or service to pay for itself. Speak about the number of minutes that can be saved, how much productivity can be increased, or how many errors will be eliminated by using the product or service.

Throughout the interest and desire sections, the writer works to make the reader want to take advantage of the product, service, or idea. Some writers are tempted to stretch the truth or make wild statements about benefits. Exaggerations make the reader lose interest in the message and think poorly of the writer. If the message is external, the image of the business can be tarnished. If the message is internal, the credibility of the writer can be questioned. The problem, however, doesn't end there. Making incomplete or false statements is unethical and can be illegal. Honesty is the best policy.

When readers have finished reading the desire section, they should ask, "What do I do next?" The answer is provided in the action section.

## Action

In this section, the writer clearly, concisely, and confidently shows what the reader must do to get the benefits described in the interest section. For example, the writer lists phone numbers; encloses reply cards or postage-paid, self-addressed envelopes; or expresses a willingness to discuss the topic. Prompt action is encouraged by offering discounts, offering to bill the reader at a later date, or setting a deadline by which action must be taken. Message unity is achieved by referring once again to the benefits the reader will receive. Goodwill is achieved by maintaining a courteous tone.

# TYPES OF PERSUASIVE MESSAGES

AIDA can be used in various types of persuasive messages, including sales messages, requests, claims, collection messages, and proposals.

## Sales Messages

Sales messages are used in business-to-business and business-to-consumer situations. A pump sales representative might write to a heavy equipment manufacturer to promote a model that has better rings than the one currently in use; the new rings would increase fluid flow. A pharmaceutical sales representative might send a form letter to physicians in her area promoting a drug shown to be effective in treating patients with Alzheimer's disease. A magazine publisher might write to all current subscribers of its travel magazine to induce them to subscribe to a new magazine about cruising. All three letters would follow the AIDA plan but the last two, typically classed as *direct mail*, would differ from the first in the following ways:

*Chapter 6: Writing Persuasive Messages*

## Desire and Action

Last year your company paid $500 to rent an 8- by 10-foot display space at a business products show. You are proposing that: (1) your company participate in the show again and (2) you double the size of your display space. The larger display area will cost $1,250.

1. What facts and figures could you present to convince your supervisor to display at the show this year?

2. Your annual advertising budget is $7,500. How can you overcome your supervisor's objection to spending one-sixth of your annual budget on one event?

3. Do you think setting a date by which your supervisor should respond is "pushy"? Why or why not?

**LENGTH.** Direct mail sales messages may exceed one page; business-to-consumer sales messages often exceed four pages. Although writers don't expect recipients to read the entire message, they hope that something in the mass of text will pique readers' interest enough that they will seek more information or decide to buy the product or service.

**ENCLOSURES.** Direct mail sales messages frequently include photos, brochures, coupons, samples, and return envelopes. The items are designed to generate interest, provide additional details, or encourage a reply.

**UNCONVENTIONAL GRAMMAR/PUNCTUATION.** Sentence fragments, exclamation points, and ellipsis points may be used to gain attention, hold interest, and achieve a conversational style. These techniques are improper in other business messages.

## "Your 'Ode To A Prospect' was the most original sales letter I've ever received."

> Getting receivers to read a sales message requires special effort.

> Some sales messages are creative; others are traditional.

**VISUAL DEVICES.** Colored paper, colored ink, unusual stationery sizes, type style/size variations, and indented text are some of the visual devices that can be used to get reader attention. The audience and situation guide the writer in determining which devices are appropriate. For example, the pharmaceutical sales representative might use a bulleted list to highlight the drug's benefits; the magazine publisher might use larger paper and color to capture reader interest.

To minimize mailing costs, direct mail sales messages are often sent via third-class bulk mail. The rapidly increasing volume of third-class mail has prompted writers to find other ways to make their messages stand out. Some try to attract readers' attention by making the envelope unique. A black envelope with white printing is distinctive. A bright orange label with FREE GIFT ENCLOSED printed on it attracts attention and encourages the reader to look inside. Captions such as *Important*, *Limited Time Offer*, and *You're a Winner* can motivate receivers to read a message.

Some writers believe readers are immune to these techniques and throw away third-class mail without opening it. Therefore, writers try to make their third-class mail look like first-class mail. Return addresses are subtle rather than bold. Individually prepared envelopes replace those with labels. Stamps are used in place of metered mail. Stationery is white, tan, or grey; and both the return and the mailing envelopes are color-coordinated with the stationery.

### WORKPLACE CONNECTION

E-mail is growing in popularity as a sales method. Often, the goal of the message is to get receivers to visit the sending organization's website to learn more and to place an order.

Many of the techniques described here have become common in both e-mail and Internet sales messages. The presentations feature several products, services, or offers with headlines to attract attention. Instead of enclosures, links to other pages are provided. Color, type choices, animation, and sound are used to draw the reader's eye. The subject line in an e-mail sales message must be written carefully to pass through spam-blocking software and to encourage readers to open the message instead of discarding it. Surf the Internet and check your e-mail for the next week, and you will find examples of these sales techniques.

## Requests

The key to writing an effective persuasive request is showing how the request benefits the reader. It is also important to include enough details to enable the reader to give the request full consideration. Figure 6-1 on page 120 shows a letter asking a businessman to host a fundraising event on his property.

Notice how the opening uses a story to which the reader can relate. The theme, helping a local library, is introduced in the opening paragraph and developed in the second. Reader benefits are also identified in this paragraph. Rather than naming all the details associated with the project—and there could be many—the writer says she will take the initiative to schedule a meeting during which those items can be discussed. The literary references (fiction/chapter) in the opening and close give the message unity.

Requests must show reader benefit and provide complete details.

## Claims

Claims may be either routine or persuasive. The difference is the anticipated reaction of the reader. If you order merchandise and it arrives in damaged condition, you expect the seller to replace it; your claim will be direct. If, however, the merchandise arrives in good condition but malfunctions after its warranty expires, you should anticipate that the manufacturer or seller will resist making repairs without charge; your request will be persuasive.

**Products and services most complained of by consumers:**

1. **Home Improvements/Repairs**
2. **Automobile Sales**
3. **Automobile Repairs**
4. **Credit**
5. **Telecommunications/Cable/Satellite**

**13th annual consumer survey, NACAA/CFA:**
**http://www.consumerfed.org/NACAAComplaintreport.pdf**

## Prospect Public Library

122 Tidewater Street • Prospect, MD 21613-2980
(301) 555-0120 • http://www.prospectlibrary.org

March 6, 200-

Mr. Walter Price
Cottage by the Lake
43 Liberty Lake Drive
Prospect, MD 21613-2846

Dear Mr. Price

**1** Imagine walking to the doors of Prospect Public Library and finding them locked . . . or asking for a best-selling novel and being told it isn't among the library's holdings. This isn't fiction, Mr. Price. These scenarios and more will become a reality unless Prospect Public Library can generate additional funds to augment its dwindling budget.

**2** Because you're an avid reader and a respected community leader, we are inviting you to host "Lap the Lake," the first and most important fundraising event planned for 200-. The tree-lined path and peaceful surroundings make Liberty Lake the perfect site for the event, and Cottage by the Lake would be an ideal spot for pre- and post-walk activities.

**3** In return for letting us use your facilities, your business name will appear on all promotional materials and registration forms. You would officiate at the start of the walk and present certificates to those who raise the most money. In addition, your name would be added to the Friends of the Library plaque displayed in the building foyer.

**4** I'll phone you within the next week to arrange a time when we can discuss the project in greater detail. I look forward to having you with us as we begin to write this new chapter in the history of Prospect Public Library.

Sincerely

*Ruth D'Onofrio*

Ruth D'Onofrio, Director

**Annotations**

**1** Gains attention by describing a problem.

**2** Builds interest by showing how the reader can help solve the problem.

**3** Creates desire by offering advertising and long-term recognition.

**4** Ends by making action easy.

**Figure 6-1**
Persuasive Request

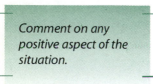

*Comment on any positive aspect of the situation.*

*Use negative words if necessary.*

Unlike routine claims, which begin with a direct statement of the problem, persuasive claims begin with one or more statements to set the context of the message. If there is some positive aspect of the situation, the opening paragraph might mention it.

In the interest section of a persuasive claim, the writer outlines the events that led to writing the message. Specific dates are helpful, but not essential. Negative words may be needed to express the writer's dissatisfaction. Explaining what inconvenience has been experienced can increase the seller's desire to remedy the situation.

After providing essential details, the writer requests an adjustment. The requested adjustment must be reasonable, and it must be stated clearly. The writer should include the date by which the receiver should respond or take action. If the writer asks the reader to telephone, he or she should include a number and a good time to make contact.

Claims should be presented calmly, clearly, and completely to have the best chance of succeeding. Messages that have an angry tone or threaten the reader are not persuasive.

Figure 6-2 shows a claim letter. This letter states the purpose of the message and gives the positive aspects of the situation early. As the message is developed, the writer gives specific details of the claim and requests definite action. A time frame for response is included, and the writer's offer to phone makes action easy.

> Request a reasonable adjustment.

> Avoid showing anger or making threats.

---

**Polen Insurance Agency**

349 Merchant Street
Emporia, KS 66801-4056  (620) 555-0183

November 2, 200-

Mr. Michael Sandeval
Sandeval Systems
224 Prairie Street
Emporia, KS 66801-9483

Dear Mr. Sandeval

[1] Last April, I purchased four Model 24B Marks air purifiers from you for use in my office. The purifiers have worked well, and my employees appreciate the way they draw allergens from the air.

[2] We have followed the manufacturer's instructions for cleaning the units and last week began a quest to find replacement filters. First, we phoned your store; then, we called the manufacturer. Much to our surprise and disappointment, we learned that the Model 24B was discontinued June 30 and that replacement filters are no longer available.

When we selected the Model 24B, you told us it was a "state-of-the-art" purifier that would meet our needs well into the future. The purifiers have met our needs but, without filters, we cannot use them now or in the future. Therefore, we request that you replace the units with another model and provide two sets of replacement filters for them. As shown on the enclosed copy of my receipt, the purifiers were not marked as closeout or discontinued merchandise, and we paid full price for them.

[3] Please phone to arrange the exchange. Let's *clear the air* on this matter within the next two weeks.

Sincerely

*Quinn Polen*

Quinn Polen
Enclosure

**Annotations**

[1] Sets context for claim and makes positive statements about the product.

[2] Describes problem.

[3] Requests specific action.

**Figure 6-2**
Persuasive Claim

## Collection Messages

Whenever a business loans money or provides services or goods on credit, there is a chance that customers will not pay their bills on time. Generally, one or more of the following conditions has prompted customers to delay their payments:

- They have simply overlooked the billing statement.

- They don't have enough money to pay the bill.

- They are dissatisfied with the service or the merchandise.

- They seldom pay on time; late or missed payments are a habit.

Regardless of the cause of the problem, businesses must try to collect. If customers don't pay, the business may be unable to meet its obligations to employees and creditors. Its profits could decline.

As important as it is to collect what it is due, business professionals realize they are dealing with people. They recognize and respect the role pride plays in collection situations. Therefore, they approach collection messages in three stages: reminder, appeal, and warning.

**REMINDER.** In the reminder stage, writers assume that readers want to pay but have simply overlooked the bill. Reminders are often light-hearted. Some commonly used tactics include a computer-generated message printed on a copy of the statement, a bright sticker on a copy of the bill, and a postcard calling attention to the unpaid bill. Figure 6-3 shows a sporting goods store's billing reminder.

Put your payments back on target . . . pay your past-due Redmond's account today.

### Figure 6-3
Collection Reminder

The number of reminders a business sends can vary with the size of the debt and the debtor's payment history. If the debt is small or the debtor has a good payment history, the number of reminders will be as high as five or six. The time between reminders can vary, too. The first reminder might not be sent until the bill is 30 days past due.

As the number of reminders increases, the time between them decreases. During the last segment of the reminder stage, messages might be sent every two or three days.

**APPEAL.** If reminders don't persuade the debtor to pay, the writer moves to the next stage, appeal. The writer carefully chooses the appeal that will have the greatest effect on the reader. The appeal could be to the reader's pride, sense of duty, desire to have good credit, or a combination of these. The appeal is introduced in the opening paragraph and developed in the middle section of the message.

The approach taken in the close depends on whether the message is in the first or last stage of appeal. At first, the writer will push for a reason why payment has been delayed. Later, the writer will ask the reader to pay something, even a small amount, against the debt. The writer can also invite the reader to call or visit to develop a repayment plan. Figure 6-4 shows a collection message in the appeal stage.

*When reminders are unsuccessful, use appeals.*

August 3, 200-

Mr. Kenneth J. Lopper
17 Pearl Street, Apt. 2
Paterson, NJ 07501-2208

Dear Mr. Lopper

**Annotations**

1 Appeal

2 Details

3 Call for Action

1 On March 17, one of our dentists gave you her immediate attention. Now, Mr. Lopper, it's time for you to give us your immediate attention.

2 When you visited our dental clinic, you were in pain. Your gums were bleeding and inflamed. Your tooth, you said, was throbbing badly. Because you required immediate care, patients who had scheduled appointments were asked to wait while Dr. Sherbloom and her assistant tended to your needs. The patient information form you completed and signed indicated that you would be responsible for the entire bill. Therefore, the bill for your care was mailed to you. Neither the bill nor the three reminders we've sent have prompted you to pay. Why, Mr. Lopper?

3 If you are unable to pay the entire $345 now, pay what you can. Then, phone me to arrange a payment plan. We want only what you owe us, Mr. Lopper . . . your immediate attention to the enclosed bill.

Yours truly

*Mark Gui*

Mark Gui
Billing Clerk

Enclosure

**PATERSON FAMILY DENTISTRY**
73 Redwood Avenue | Paterson, NJ 07522-1925 | (973) 555-0146

**Figure 6-4**
Appeal Stage Collection Letter

*When gentler attempts to collect fail, issue a warning.*

**WARNING.** In the warning stage, the writer *demands* action. Several weeks, perhaps months, have passed. Gentle reminders and polite requests have failed. The only tactic left is strength. The writer clearly and honestly presents the action that will be taken if payment is not received. A short deadline is set before the debt is referred to a lawyer or collection agency. Figure 6-5 shows a warning stage collection message.

## Proposals

*Proposals offer solutions to problems.*

A business proposal is a special, more advanced type of persuasive message. It is designed to define and offer a solution to a problem.

October 1, 200-

Mr. Kenneth J. Lopper
17 Pearl Street, Apt. 2
Paterson, NJ 07501-2208

Dear Mr. Lopper

You've given us no choice. Your account must be referred to a collection agency.

We didn't want this to happen, Mr. Lopper; did you? We acted in good faith when we provided you with the emergency dental care you needed on March 17. We believed you would pay us for the professional care you received. We were wrong. You've ignored bills, reminders, and appeals for payment.

If you haven't paid us the $345 you owe by October 7, we will refer your account to the Brothers Agency. It's your choice, Mr. Lopper.

Yours truly

*Mark Gui*

Mark Gui
Billing clerk

PATERSON FAMILY DENTISTRY
73 Redwood Avenue | Paterson, NJ 07522-1925 | (973) 555-0146

**Figure 6-5**
Warning Stage Collection Letter

## TYPES OF BUSINESS PROPOSALS.

Proposals may be internal or external and solicited or unsolicited.

*Internal.* These proposals are designed to solve a problem within an organization. Procedure changes, policy modifications, equipment acquisitions, and employee incentives are examples of internal proposal topics. Internal proposals, which may be submitted as memos or reports, are directed to managers or management/staff teams that have the authority to approve and fund them.

*External.* These proposals are written for an audience outside the organization. Readers could be affiliated with a foundation or other philanthropic group, a government agency, or a for-profit organization such as a bank. Establishing a new seniors' center, sponsoring an afternoon reading program for elementary school students, and conducting research related to cancer are examples of external proposal topics. The business plan an entrepreneur submits to a financial institution or group of investors also falls into this category. External proposals, which will be reviewed by panels within or outside the funding source, can be formatted as letters or reports.

*Solicited.* These proposals are written in response to a **request for proposal (RFP)** or **request for bid (RFB)**. The request gives specific information about what will be funded or purchased, guidelines to be followed in preparing the proposal or bid, and information about when and to whom to send the completed document. Some RFPs also require the writer to complete and submit an application form.

*Unsolicited.* These proposals are submitted solely on the writer's initiative. In a business environment, a worker might submit an outline or text summary of a proposal and then meet with a manager to get an indication of whether she or he is aware of a problem or is receptive to a particular solution. If the manager says, "Expand it and put it in writing," a detailed written proposal is prepared. External agencies sometimes encourage groups to submit pre-proposals before developing full proposals.

## PARTS OF A BUSINESS PROPOSAL.

Every proposal contains some or all of the following parts depending on its purpose and audience:

*Title.* The proposal title should be brief and descriptive. Try to keep the title to ten or fewer words. Use action verbs and nouns. A creative title can capture a reader's attention.

*Abstract or Executive Summary.* This section provides an overview of the subject, purpose, activities, and expected outcomes of the proposal. A paragraph of 200 to 250 words and 10 to 15 sentences will acquaint readers with the topic and stimulate interest in it.

> *Proposals can have one or several readers.*

> *An introductory or pre-proposal can be useful.*

**Introduction and Problem Statement.** These parts can be presented separately or in one section. The introduction should give a sense of the problem and its history. It should establish a need and hold the readers' interest. A literature review or results of a pilot project would also be included in this section. The problem statement should provide a conceptual, broad-based framework for the goals of the project. *Employee retention* is an example of a problem. When phrased as a problem statement in a proposal, details are added for context, as in this example:

> During fiscal year 2006, our attrition among nursing assistants was 18 percent, nearly double the industry average of 11 percent.

**Objectives.** The specific, achievable, measurable outcomes of the proposal are its objectives. *Increase retention of nursing assistants by 25 percent by the end of the fiscal year* is an objective.

**Methods/Activities.** This section describes your implementation procedures. It answers the questions *what? when?* and *why?* A well-organized action plan can boost the readers' desire to fund the project.

**Evaluation.** Show readers that you are serious about assessing outcomes and making appropriate modifications to ensure success. State what data you plan to gather and when they will be collected. Tell readers how you will analyze the data and report results. Focus on continuous improvement.

**Budget.** Readers will want to know how you plan to spend their money. Include cost estimates for personnel (salaries, fringe benefits) and other needs (space, equipment, supplies, travel). Be honest and realistic. Do not inflate or understate expenses. Identify confirmed funding sources if you have them.

**Future Funding.** Tell readers how you plan to fund the project after the requested funds have been depleted.

**Appendices.** Background information or supporting documents should be presented as appendices. Keep the text of the proposal brief and focused.

**Personnel.** Include brief résumés for people who are involved with the project. Show readers that you and your collaborators have the qualifications to make what you propose happen.

In long, formal proposals, each of these items could be displayed as a separate section. In letter or memo proposals, side headings can be used to guide the reader from section to section. Figure 6-6 shows a memo proposal.

> *The Kellogg Foundation is able to fund only a very small percentage of the requests it currently receives. Many requests are declined, not because they are lacking in merit, but because they do not match our current programming interests or programming guidelines.*
>
> —http://www.wkkf.org/ Grants/Process.aspx

*Chapter 6: Writing Persuasive Messages*

| TO: | Arthur Lofdahl, Owner | ✦ *One Park Place* |
|---|---|---|
| FROM: | Ellen Husset, Manager *eh* | |
| DATE: | June 6, 200- | |
| SUBJECT: | Reallocation of Lobby Space | |

On a typical day, more than 3,000 people pass through the lobby of One Park Place, many of them carrying a cup of hot coffee. We could provide a service to those tenants and their clients by installing a coffee kiosk in our lobby.

**Background**

More than 50 percent of Americans over age 18 drink coffee daily. About one-third of the coffee-drinking public consumes a specialty coffee beverage each day.

**Problem**

The fourth-floor cafeteria serves only regular and decaffeinated coffee and doesn't have space to brew flavored coffees or make espresso. Therefore, our tenants and their clients who want something other than basic coffee must go elsewhere to purchase their beverages.

The nearest specialty coffee shop is four blocks west of One Park Place, which makes it inconvenient for tenants and guests. In addition, carrying coffee through crowded streets or while toting a briefcase or package can be messy. Last Tuesday, I observed four coffee spills before 7:30 a.m.

**Recommendation**

I recommend that we reallocate lobby space to accommodate a freestanding coffee kiosk and seating for 10–15 customers. Specifically, I recommend we pursue one of the following options (prioritized):

- Offer our cafeteria food management company the opportunity to lease the space to operate a kiosk.

- Solicit lease/operate kiosk bids from independent vendors.

- Install and operate the kiosk ourselves.

After researching the topic, I am confident we can provide this service with little or no remodeling. If you concur that this service will distinguish our property from others in the area, I'd appreciate the opportunity to discuss the details and cost comparisons with you. If we act within the next month, we can have the service available by October 1.

**Figure 6-6**
Unsolicited Memo Proposal

# Proposal Elements

Create the following for a proposal to implement a program to reduce the number of workplace injuries experienced by warehouse workers.

Title:

Problem Statement:

Objective:

Methods/Activities:

Evaluation:

**BUSINESS PLANS.** A business plan is a special-purpose proposal submitted to a financial institution to secure the funding necessary to create or expand a business. The components of a business plan are similar to those of a proposal:

*Introduction/Summary.* This section gives a concise description of the business and its proposed location, states how much funding you need and why, and identifies the time period for which money is needed.

*Ownership/Management/Employee Data.* This section describes the proposed structure of the business and provides information about the experience, skills, training, and qualifications of key personnel.

*Product/Service/Market Identification.* Products and services are described and differentiated from the competition's. The market is defined, and a marketing strategy is presented. Sales forecasts based on market research, actual or expected orders, and comparative pricing are provided.

*Administration/Production Factors.* This section offers information about equipment and facilities, production techniques, quality control mechanisms, management structure, and accounting systems and controls.

*Growth and Development Plans and Potential.* This section makes a one- or two-year projection linked to improvement or expansion of products, services, or markets; changes in required staffing; and additional investment.

*Financial Information.* This section explains how much the project will cost, what will be provided, what is needed, and what financial security you can offer lenders.

*Appendices.* Appendices include documents that relate to the plan or further explain or support it.

When developing a business plan, entrepreneurs often seek the assistance of business development professionals. Universities, chambers of commerce, and government-sponsored economic development agencies frequently provide low-cost or free assistance. To learn more about preparing a business plan and to see samples, visit one of the following websites:

- http://www.sba.gov/starting_business/planning/basic.html
- http://www.businessplans.org
- http://www.bplans.com/sp/businessplans.cfm

## Keys to Writing Effective Proposals and Business Plans

Proposals, like other forms of business writing, should reflect the 4Cs of business communication and show evidence of thorough planning.

# WORKPLACE CONNECTION

Ask someone who is unfamiliar with the proposal to read it for completeness and clarity.

In addition, proposals should:

- Strictly adhere to the guidelines of the funding agency.
- Use side heads and clear transitions to guide the reader.
- Use lists to break up text and highlight important points.
- Keep visuals to a minimum; use them only to enhance and explain abstract concepts and relationships.
- Address potential problems, not avoid them.
- Avoid using jargon unless the terms have been precisely defined.
- Show genuine enthusiasm for the project.
- Be free of typographical, grammatical, and content errors.

## CHAPTER SUMMARY

- Persuasive messages are written using the indirect approach.
- For persuasive messages, the indirect approach uses the AIDA plan (attention, interest, desire, and action).
- Persuasive messages include sales messages, requests, claims, collection messages, and proposals.
- Sales messages sent to consumers differ from other persuasive messages in length and in the use of enclosures, unconventional grammar/punctuation, and visual devices.
- Requests should stress reader benefit and should include enough details for the reader to give the request full consideration.
- Persuasive claims state the problem, stress any positive aspect of the situation, outline its history, and ask for a reasonable adjustment.
- Collection messages progress through three stages: reminder, appeal, and warning.
- Proposals define and offer a solution to a problem.
- Proposals may be internal or external and either solicited or unsolicited.
- A proposal consists of the following parts: title, abstract or executive summary, introduction and problem statement, objectives, methods/activities, evaluation, budget, future funding, appendices, and personnel.
- A business plan is a special-purpose proposal consisting of an introduction/summary, ownership/management/employee data, product/service/market identification, administration/production factors, growth and development plans and potential, financial information, and appendices.
- Effective proposals and business plans adhere to the principles of good writing.

## Section I: Work-Related Messages

The following exercises require you to apply the indirect approach in writing work-related messages. Read the directions carefully. Unless your instructor tells you otherwise, use the style you prefer for memos or letters. Use today's date, and invent reasonable details as necessary. Apply the 4Cs of communication that you learned about in Chapter 3, and remember to proofread your messages for mechanics.

1. You have been hired to raise money to restore the Avalon Theater in your town. The people you work for plan to overhaul the 90-year-old theater, which has been empty for nearly a decade. The plan is to convert the old theater into a forum for American and foreign films, concerts, and live theater performances. You are ready to ask residents to contribute money to fix the Avalon's seats. A contribution of $45 will restore one seat. Your task is to write a message asking people to restore one or more of the seats or to donate whatever they can to the project. Those who contribute $45 or more will receive a $15 reduction in the cost of a season ticket to the first year's events.

   a.  Who will read your message?

   b.  What appeal(s) will you use?

   c.  What ideas will you use to generate interest?

   d.  What details will you use to build desire?

   e.  What action will you ask for?

   f.  Will you set a deadline for action? If yes, what?

   g.  Are enclosures needed? If so, what?

   h.  Using the notes you made in items a–g above, write the message on a separate sheet of paper.

## Sales Messages

2. You are a real estate agent who wants to increase the number of houses you sell. Each time you sell a home, you write to other homeowners in the area asking whether they are interested in selling their homes and encouraging them to work with you. Prepare the form letter you will use. Your company offers clients the following services: market evaluation, open houses, and advertising.

3. Your company, Rigsbee Orchards, places flyers like the one below next to the cash register in its store. The flyers have created some interest in your products, but not enough. You recently suggested that sales letters be prepared and sent to businesses listed with the local Chamber of Commerce. Your supervisor liked the idea and has asked you to draft the message. Do so, and e-mail it to your instructor.

*Rigsbee Orchards*
*400 S. West Street*
*Greenfield, IN 46140-2245*

Here are just a FEW of the MANY gift ideas
for customers, employees, and associates
from RIGSBEE ORCHARDS

**#25 The Morning Glory** ($8)
Two 12-oz bottles of syrup: one blueberry, one blackberry.

**#26 The Two-Tea Fruity** ($6)
A 2-oz jar of raspberry jam and two packages of raspberry tea.

**#27 The Fruit Fancy** ($14)
A 6-oz package of blueberry pancake mix, a 10-oz package of blueberry muffin mix, and a 12-oz bottle of blueberry syrup.

**#28 Deluxe Berry Basket** ($20)
Two jams (2 oz each) and two syrups (12 oz each) of your choice (strawberry, cherry, blueberry, blackberry, raspberry).

## We can

➔ **customize** any gift with your personalized message.
➔ **handle** any and all shipping arrangements.
➔ **guarantee** delivery by the date you choose.
➔ **include** your logo and/or company name.
    (317) 555-0110

4. Your friend Cami Earl recently opened a catering business (Catering by Cami) and is trying to develop a client base. Last month she participated in a regional bridal fair. At the conclusion of the event, vendors were given the names and addresses of those who attended. Cami has removed the names of people who registered at her booth and will contact each individually. She's asked for your help in preparing a form message that she could send attendees who didn't register at her booth to persuade them to consider her as their caterer.

5. The message you wrote in Application 4 was so successful that Cami has asked you to help her again. This time, she wants to promote her boxed lunches—an assortment of delicious and healthful sandwiches, salads, and beverages—as a choice for on-site meetings. Cami believes her willingness to deliver the lunches is a key selling point. Your audience is members of the local Chamber of Commerce.

6. Since you were eight years old, you've had an interest in and talent for magic. So, to support yourself while you're in college, you've decided to develop a magic act and perform at birthday parties, festivals, and other evening and weekend gatherings. Write a letter that you can use to promote your services.

## Requests

7. You are a health care professional at a 300-bed regional hospital, and you are concerned that the hospital hasn't done enough to respond to research that cites obesity as a severe problem among the American population. The cafeteria has made changes in its menu and has posted nutritional information for many of the items it offers. All too often, though, employees and visitors make quick selections from the vending machines located on each floor and "eat on the run." Write to Brenda Asleson, the hospital administrator, and persuade her to replace the soda and snack machines with ones that offer fruit, sandwiches, and juices.

8. A policy at your company states that employees who have been with the firm one year are entitled to one week of paid vacation and those who have been with the firm two to five years get two weeks' paid vacation. Your two-year anniversary isn't until November 12, but you hope to persuade your employer to permit you to take your two-week vacation October 23–November 6 so you can go to Ireland to compete in the Dublin Marathon. Write an e-mail to Curtis Matthews, your supervisor.

9. You work part-time at the local zoo. It's late December, and your supervisor is planning programs for next year. In the past, the zoo has sponsored a successful Groundhog Day event, one that attracted local media coverage. Unfortunately, the zoo's groundhog died in September, and the director has not yet located a replacement. Your supervisor (DeWayne James) wants to cancel the Groundhog Day event. Persuade him to conduct the event using Pete the Porcupine as a replacement.

10. The fax machine in your office needs to be replaced. Do the research necessary to persuade your manager to purchase a particular make and model. Prepare an appropriate memo.

11. Your community hosts an in-line skating marathon (26.2 miles) each June. Hundreds of volunteers are needed to make the event a success. Volunteers are needed to:

- Work at the registration tables.
- Issue T-shirts to the finishers.
- Serve water at the rest stops.
- Work at the post-race refreshment tent.
- Take numbers at the finish line.

The local newspaper has donated a quarter-page ad in the sports section and will print your message calling for volunteers. As staff coordinator for the race, write the message.

12. You are an active member of an association related to your field of study. Your local chapter (Norristown, PA) will host the organization's regional conference this spring. Your task is to get items to put in the hospitality packets that will be given to each person who attends the regional meeting. The Krispy Potato Chip Company is based in Norristown at 1250 Powell Street, 19401-3301. Write to request that they donate 300 packages of their chocolate-covered ripple chips.

13. Write a message persuading the mayor of your community to spend an hour in the dunk tank at the city festival on July 4.

## Claims

14. The hotel stay associated with your recent business trip was plagued with problems. The reservation request you faxed to the hotel clearly showed you expected to arrive for your one-night stay at 2 a.m. on June 10. The confirmation notice you received also showed June 10, but when you tried to check in, you were told there were no rooms available and you should have listed June 9 as your arrival date. After a lengthy discussion with the night manager, you were given a room with the hope that the person who had really reserved it didn't arrive. You had a fitful night's sleep because of the constant traffic to and from the vending and ice machines located near your room. You phoned the desk to complain but were told that hotel guests have a right to use the vending machines. You didn't have time to talk to the hotel manager before you left for your meetings the next day. Write a request for a refund of the $148.95 you paid for your room. The address is Travelers' Best Hotel, 615 Texas Street, Houston, TX 77002-2710.

15. The printer delivered 4,000 copies of your company's annual report this morning. Much to your disappointment, the colors are not as vivid as you expected them to be, and the graphs appear to have light shadows behind the lines. The reports are scheduled to be mailed to shareholders in ten days. Neither problem was detectable in the proofs you approved; other projects completed with this printer have been excellent. Persuade the printer to redo the reports at no charge. The address is Magnuson Printers, 109 N. Market Street, Wilmington, DE 19801-2525.

16. Last year, your company bought five industrial vacuum cleaners for your custodial staff. Yesterday, the staff supervisor told you that cords on two of the machines were frayed because of a defect in the rewind mechanism. When he tried to order replacement rewind units, which were not covered under warranty, he learned they were no longer made. You agree with his conclusion that parts should be available for machines that are less than a year old. Write a claim to the manufacturer, Prescott Vacuums, 1305 Barton Road, Pocatello, ID 83204-1847.

17. On July 17, you accepted a bid from Chesley Cleaning Services to shampoo the carpets in your four-room office suite. Rex Alther, the representative with whom you met, indicated that the work would be done by August 1 and that he would phone three days in advance to make final arrangements. You gave him a $100 deposit on the $750 job. When you hadn't heard from Mr. Alther by July 28, you phoned the company and learned that he quit on July 18. Although your check has not been cashed, you believe that the company should honor the commitment Mr. Alther made while he was an employee. Write the owner, Florence Harrington, asking that the work be completed by August 31 and that you be billed for only $600— the original fee less the deposit and $50 for your inconvenience. The company's address is 841 Jackson Boulevard, Rapid City, SD 57702-2529.

## Collection Messages

18. Clay Reynolds has been shopping at your family-owned clothing store for more than 40 years. Three months ago, he bought a suit and accessories to wear at his granddaughter's wedding. You haven't seen him since. He hasn't paid the $547 bill or responded to the reminders you've sent. You've tried phoning, but no one answers and there is no answering machine. Prepare an appeal stage message. Mr. Reynolds' address is 301 N. Wood Circle, Cedar City, UT 84720-2076.

19. Refer to Application 6. Two weeks ago, you performed your magic act at Samantha Lehrke's tenth birthday party. The 15 children who attended enjoyed your performance, as did Samantha's parents, Audrey and Ellis. In fact, they invited you to stay for cake and ice cream, which you did. As you left, you gave Ellis your bill, which indicated payment was due in ten days. You haven't yet received payment. Prepare a reminder message. The Lehrkes' address is 801 Lincoln Avenue, Aiken, SC 29801-3487.

20. In response to a collection appeal you wrote, Harlan Spacey arranged to pay the $1,800 he owed you for carpentry work in six monthly installments of $300. In consideration of his efforts, you agreed to waive interest on the debt. Mr. Spacey made the first two payments on time; his third payment was a week late. You have heard nothing from him in the eight weeks since that payment was due, even though you left him four courteous voice-mail messages and sent him two letters. Your patience has been exhausted. Notify Mr. Spacey that you are referring his account to a collection agency. His address is 531 Sands Circle, Reidville, NC 27320-4025.

21. The computer-generated bills that your company sends each month have space for messages. You've decided to use the space to thank customers who pay on time and to remind customers when their bills are past due. Write the friendly reminder you will include on accounts that are 30 to 60 days past due. Limit the reminder to 200 characters.

## Proposals

22. Working in teams of three or four as directed by your instructor, identify a problem at your school and prepare a proposal to solve it.

23. Every year, your company buys a block of 20 season tickets for a professional sporting team's events. Tickets are available to employees at no charge. Propose to Beth Mears, the human resource manager, that a similar program be enacted for the local symphony.

24. The school district for which you work as business manager is experiencing severe budget problems. In order to retain as many programs and personnel as possible, the superintendent, Wagner Clarkson, has asked employees to recommend changes that will yield savings—even modest ones. Propose that the district send thank-you notes only for contributions of $100 or more. Currently, thank-you notes are sent for all donations, even those in the $1 to $5 range.

25. Job sharing, flextime, and telecommuting are three programs that have gained popularity in recent years. Select one and prepare a preliminary proposal memo that supports its adoption in the organization where you work. Do an Internet search to identify sources of information and list them in your proposal.

26. The pet shelter where you volunteer needs new dog runs. Write a letter proposal asking a local fence supplier to donate the materials and labor to install the runs. The address is Laperty Fencing, 40 Willow Street, Waterbury, CT 06710-2003.

# Section II: Personal-Business Messages

The following exercises relate to using the indirect approach in writing situations you might face in your personal life. Read the directions carefully. Use the personal-business letter format. Use today's date, and invent reasonable details as necessary. Apply the 4Cs of good communication presented in Chapter 3. Plan before you write, and proofread for mechanics.

27. You have been invited to join the local chapter of Alpha Beta Gamma (ABG), an active group for business professionals. Each chapter has a membership limit of 25; the last time the local chapter accepted a member was in 2002. According to the invitation, signed by Membership Chair E. Jacob Zenk, the initiation ceremony—which new members *must* attend—is scheduled for February 20. As sales manager for Falls Industries, you travel frequently. In fact, you will be out of town February 19–22, meeting with an important client. You really want to join this group . . . so much so that you will attempt to persuade the group to modify its initiation procedures. ABG's address is 246 S. Mason Road, St. Louis, MO 63141-8027.

28. Assume your school selects one student a year as its "Outstanding Graduate." Nominate a classmate for the award. Address your message to the Selection Committee.

29. Last night you attended a local theater's production of *Fiddler on the Roof*. Normally, productions at the playhouse are excellent . . . not this time. The sound system crackled during four of the musical numbers, the air conditioner wasn't working, and you snagged the sleeve of your jacket on the ragged edge of the seat arm. You were so angry that you left at the intermission. You still haven't calmed down. You paid $17.50 for your ticket, and you want a refund. Write to the ticket office manager and state your claim. The address is Pressley Theater, One W. 15th Avenue, Eugene, OR 97401-4001.

30. Enough is enough! For the third time this year, your favorite TV show has been switched to a new day and time. Write to the network program planner to express your dissatisfaction and persuade him or her to move the show back to one of its earlier time slots. The address is TZT Network, Inc., 12 W. 55th Street, New York, NY 10019-5356.

31. Last night you fixed a "Spicy Chicken and Rice" dinner that had been in your freezer for at least two months. When you lifted the lid, you noticed that the dinner had very little chicken; when you took the first bite, you discovered the dinner tasted bland. The *Sell* by date on the dinner was ten days ago. Write the manufacturer to express your disappointment and request a refund. You no longer have the sales slip but think you paid $2.89 for the dinner. The address is Barkis Frozen Foods, 347 Union Avenue, Bakersfield, CA 93307-1554.

32. You purchased a royal blue chenille sweater as a birthday gift for your sister. Once you determined the sweater fit, you disposed of your receipt. Now, two months later, your sister comments that the sweater is shedding. She repeatedly finds blue "fuzzies" on her purse and backpack after she's worn the sweater. In addition, the chenille is nearly gone from the areas where her arms rub against her sides as she walks. The sweater has held its color well during washing and hasn't shrunk. You paid $40 for the sweater and think it should be more durable than what your sister reports. You took the sweater back to the store where you bought it, but the clerk with whom you spoke said you would have to submit a written claim to the store manager, Brett Sauter. The address is 102 Main Street, Franconia, NH 03580-4814.

# Writing Employment and Special Messages

Taping a résumé to the inside cover of a boxed pizza delivered to a prospective employer or wearing an oversized T-shirt imprinted with an occupational goal may work for some job seekers (*303 Off-the-Wall Ways to Get a Job* by Brandon Toropov), but most people find that an application letter and résumé, submitted in print or electronic form, is a better approach. Those more traditional methods are described in this chapter.

## EMPLOYMENT COMMUNICATION

People must use both written and oral communication to get jobs. Written communication consists of résumés, application letters, and other employment-related correspondence. Oral communication consists of interviews and other discussions in person or by phone. This chapter focuses on the written communication aspects of the employment process and briefly touches on a trend in business employment communication, portfolios. This chapter assumes that you have done a self-assessment to identify your interests, skills, abilities, values, goals, and personal qualities and that you have explored career options.*

## Résumés

A **résumé** is a description of an applicant's qualifications for employment. It introduces the applicant to the prospective employer and provides evidence to convince the reader that the applicant is competent to become an employee. A solicited résumé should address all items included in an employer's position announcement or job listing. When unsolicited, a résumé should highlight qualifications as they relate to a professional goal. The content and format of a résumé may vary, but all résumés have the following characteristics:

■ *Résumés have no title.* A title is unnecessary; the reader will recognize the document.

---

## LEARNING OBJECTIVES

■ Write a résumé that high-lights your strengths.

■ Compose an application letter that focuses on your qualifications.

■ Write other messages associated with employment communication.

■ Learn when and how to write goodwill messages.

■ Prepare meeting minutes.

■ Write news releases.

## WORKPLACE CONNECTION

Update your résumé at least once a year—better yet, revise it each time a relevant change occurs.

---

\* For more complete coverage of employment, refer to *The Basics: Employment Communication* (0-538-69028-3).

**Research shows that managers skim résumés for about 30 seconds.**

- *Résumés are brief.* Employers skim rather than read résumés, so writers present information in phrases rather than complete sentences. A one-page résumé is typical for an entry-level job seeker. Experienced applicants should try to limit résumés to two pages.

- *Résumés are grammatically correct.* Use the present tense for current activities and the past tense for previous activities. Use parallel structure within lists.

- *Résumés are positive.* Highlight strengths. Choose words carefully.

- *Résumés stress transferable skills.* Skills can be gained through education, experience, or activities.

- *Résumés omit personal data.* Omit age, height, weight, marital status, parental status, race, gender, religious affiliation, and other items that are not related to the job or the organization.

- *Résumés provide evidence.* Give concrete examples to illustrate strengths. For example, working 20–30 hours a week while attending school and raising a family shows good time management skills. It also indicates that the applicant is responsible and ambitious.

Although a résumé should be unique to the person it represents, readers expect to find certain items in every résumé they receive.

**WORKPLACE CONNECTION**

Prospective employers will judge a candidate not only by what's posted directly to his or her personal website but also by the links listed there.

**OPENING.** The opening is the first item in a résumé. It consists of two essential parts and one optional part. Contact information and a job objective are required; a summary of qualifications is optional.

- *Contact Information.* The applicant's name, mailing address, e-mail address, and phone number(s) are standard entries. If appropriate, include current and permanent mailing addresses and the date on which a change in residence will occur. The URL for the writer's personal website may be included if its design or content is relevant to the job. A work e-mail address and phone number should be listed only if the employer permits receiving personal messages while on the job. The website and all voice-mail greetings must be professional. Figure 7-1 shows an example of contact information that includes current and permanent mailing addresses.

---

**RAY HAMBLIN**

| **Address Through May 31, 200-** | 608.555.0126 | **Permanent Address** |
| --- | --- | --- |
| 45 Richard Street | rayhamb1@continental.net | 100 W.MacArthur Avenue |
| Verona, WI 53593-1108 | | Eau Claire, WI 54701-6321 |

**Figure 7-1**
Contact Information

- *Job Objective*. A **job objective** is a brief statement that indicates the type of job the applicant wants. The objective is a critical résumé part, and everything that follows should support it. The objective may be general or targeted to a specific job or company. An objective that is too specific may prevent the applicant from being considered for employment in a related area. An objective that is too general may result in the résumé being set aside because it is vague. Statements such as *willing to travel or willing to relocate* can be linked to the objective.

**Objective:**  Summer accounting internship in a government agency or not-for-profit organization.

**Objective:**  Computer networking position in the CIS department of a progressive firm; willing to relocate.

*A word-processed résumé can be easily customized for different jobs.*

---

## [ THINKING IT THROUGH 7-1 ]

## Assessing Job Objectives

Are the following job objectives weak or strong? Why?

**1.** Objective:  Medical office assistant position.

**2.** Objective:  Medical office assistant position in Denver family practice clinic that offers advancement opportunities.

**3.** Objective:  Medical office assistant position in a clinic environment that will draw on my computer, accounting, and interpersonal communication skills to benefit both physicians and patients.

- *Summary of Qualifications.* This optional section provides the reader with an abstract of the applicant's qualifications near the start of the résumé. The summary is prepared after the rest of the entries to help the writer select only the most important items. Figure 7-2 shows an example of a summary of qualifications.

**EDUCATION.** This section presents information about postsecondary school diplomas, certificates, or degrees and when and where they were earned. Writers may include data about courses if they relate to the job being sought. Grades or grade point averages should be listed if they reflect positively on the applicant. Always put grades in context by indicating whether they reflect overall performance or performance in your field of study. Also, indicate the scale (e.g., 3.0/4.0 scale). For most recent graduates, education will be the strongest qualification; therefore, it should appear before experience.

**WORK OR OTHER EXPERIENCE.** List jobs you have held. Include the name and location of the organization, employment dates, and job titles. Describe duties, responsibilities, and accomplishments.

Workers who have had experience related to the job they are applying for as well as unrelated work experience may use separate headings, such as *Related Work Experience* and *Other Work Experience.* An entry such as *Full- and part-time jobs as food service worker, clerk,* and *lawn care worker* combines experiences to emphasize adaptability. In this case, specific details such as the names and locations of the organizations are omitted.

**SPECIAL SKILLS.** Special skills may be listed separately or as part of either education or experience. Include computer, foreign language, or other skills that an employer would expect or that could set you apart from other applicants.

**ACTIVITIES AND INTERESTS.** Memberships, leadership roles, hobbies, and accomplishments add zest to a résumé and can attract an employer's interest. If you have limited work experience, this section can also demonstrate employability skills. Try to show a balance among school, civic, and personal interests and between individual and group activities. This section is optional and should be brief.

> Omit high school information unless some aspect of it strengthens your qualifications.

> Use bullets to highlight entries.

> Activities and interests show you are a well-rounded person.

---

### Summary of Qualifications

- Accounting degree
- Accounts receivable experience
- Computer proficiency
- Exposure to enterprise systems
- Communicate effectively
- Fluentin Spanish

**Figure 7-2**
Summary of Qualifications

*Chapter 7: Writing Employment and Special Messages*

**REFERENCES.** **References** are people who can tell a potential employer about your skills, abilities, and work habits. Past or present employers, coworkers, and teachers are often used as references. It is both professional and courteous to ask permission before listing people as references.

The trend is to provide reference information only when asked. The statement *References available upon request* is optional. Some people believe it is not needed because employers already know to ask for references. Others think it represents a logical end to the document.

## Résumé Formats

The term *format* is used to describe the way a résumé is organized as well as its general appearance. Résumés can be organized using a reverse chronological, functional, or combination approach. Figures 7-3 and 7-4 on pages 143 and 144 show the first two of these methods. Note that each résumé is designed to highlight the strengths of the applicant. Résumés may be prepared as traditional paper résumés, scannable paper résumés, or online résumés.

**REVERSE CHRONOLOGICAL.** This is the most traditional and widely used résumé format. College recruiters and most employers find it attractive because it presents information in a familiar sequence, one that allows them to compare applicants easily. Entries within each section are listed from present to past to highlight academic development and professional advancement. Skills and accomplishments are displayed in bulleted vertical lists.

**FUNCTIONAL.** In functional résumés, section titles reflect the functions the applicant has performed (*merchandising, supervision, budget management*) or the traits he or she will bring to the job (*reliable, motivated, budget-conscious, creative*). The focus of this résumé is qualifications, not timing; therefore, supporting evidence is drawn from across the applicant's education, work experience, and volunteer experience without stating specifically when or where it was acquired. Brief education and employment sections are presented near the end of the résumé to provide a context for the skills and accomplishments highlighted earlier in the document. People who have changed jobs often, who are returning to the workforce after an extended absence, or who want to change career direction find this style useful.

**COMBINATION.** As the name implies, this format combines the features of reverse chronological and functional résumés. Sections are labeled and entries are sequenced as in a reverse chronological résumé; details are provided in paragraphs rather than in bulleted lists. This format works well for entry-level workers with limited experience.

## TRADITIONAL PAPER RÉSUMÉ.

Traditional résumés are simple, yet attractive. Text is set in one or two columns, in a popular, readable 10- or 12-point font. Headings, usually in larger, bold type, organize the résumé into sections. Bulleted lists stress skills and accomplishments. White or empty space sets off text attractively. Traditional résumés can have many different designs as long as they are attractive and professional.

Traditional paper résumés are most often prepared on 20-pound, 8 1/2- × 11-inch bond white paper. Some writers use off-white, ivory, light tan, or light gray. The printer chosen should be capable of producing high-quality black text. Two-sided printing is unacceptable.

## SCANNABLE PAPER RÉSUMÉ.

The first screening of a résumé may be done by human readers or by scanning software. When you know a résumé will be scanned or are not sure which method will be used, a scannable paper résumé (Figure 7-5) is the best choice. This résumé is a dual-purpose, hard-copy document designed to be visually appealing to a human reader and easily scannable by computer software.

A scannable résumé is formatted simply so that it can be scanned correctly and processed by résumé-tracking programs. Scannable résumés are best prepared using a 12-point font with distinctly separate characters (e.g., Arial or Times). Italic, script, and underscored text should be avoided; bold and all-capital letters should be used sparingly. Bullets, if used, should be solid and followed by one blank space. Applicants should use standard-size white bond paper and black ink.

Unlike traditional paper résumés, which focus on action verbs, scannable résumés include **keywords**, nouns that represent skills or qualities sought for a particular job. Résumé scanning software uses keywords entered by the employer to select the résumés the employer will actually read. Tracking software, which pulls résumés from a pool maintained for future job openings, works the same way.

Examples of keywords are *auditing*, *design*, *manager*, *leadership*, *manufacturing*, *outreach*, *trainer*, and the names of software programs and computer platforms. To learn what keywords to include in your résumé, read job ads, job descriptions, trade journals, and company websites.

## ONLINE RÉSUMÉ.

The online résumé (also called an electronic résumé) is designed to be sent in the text of an e-mail, posted to a potential employer's website, or delivered via an Internet résumé service. This résumé must be stripped of all word processing codes and is, therefore, a plain-looking document. A summary of qualifications should be placed near the top so the receiver will see it without having to scroll.

Before posting your résumé to a public site, read the privacy policy. Some professionals recommend maintaining privacy by including an e-mail address rather than a residential address in the opening. Keep track of the sites where you post your résumé, and remember to delete it when you have concluded your job search.

---

*Traditional résumés use **action verbs**, such as built, coordinated, led, managed, prepared, and presented.*

*Scannable résumés stress nouns.*

*Employers who advertise job openings online often accept applications online.*

*An online résumé may contain links to samples of your work.*

*Chapter 7: Writing Employment and Special Messages*

# Justine Schneiderman

2401 W. College Ave., Apt. 3　　　　　　　　　　　　　　303.555.0165
Denver, CO 80219-6000　　　　　　　　　　　　　schne381@rockymt.net

**OBJECTIVE**　　　Entry-level cutsomer-service position in a financial institution that encourages career development and provides advancement opportunities.

**EDUCATION**　　　A.S. degree in Business expected May 2006
Peak Community College, Denver, CO
GPA 3.0 (overall) 3.1 (major) / 4.0 scale

**RELATED EXPERIENCE**　　Teller (Internship)　　　　　　　　　　　Summer 2005
Rocky Mountain Bank, Aurora, CO
- Provided high-quality customer service
- Maintained and accurately reconciled cash drawer
- Used Vertex computer system
- Implemented theft management procedures
- Responded to questions about bank's products

**OTHER EXPERIENCE**　　Hostess/Server　　　　　　　　　　　　2003–present
Sullivan's Steak House, Denver, CO
- Greeted guests; maintained balanced seating
- Created a friendly, relaxing atmosphere for guests
- Promoted daily specials
- Processed orders courteously, quickly, and accurately
- Developed strong interpersonal communication skills
* Named *Employee of the Month* five times

Custodial Assistant　　　　　　　　　　　　　2004–2005
Peak Community College, Denver, CO
- Cleaned and sanitized facilities
- Operated industrial cleaning equipment
- Prioritized tasks and budgeted time effectively
* Nominated for Outstanding Student Employee Award

Summer jobs as camp counselor, stable hand, and babysitter

**ACTIVITIES/ INTERESTS**　　Member, Business Club
Member, Concert Choir
Volunteer, Special Olympics
Enjoy horseback riding and hiking

**REFERENCES**　　Available upon request

**Figure 7-3**
Reverse Chronological Résumé

Qualifications of
MYRON BAKER WILSON
for the position of
SALES REPRESENTATIVE with ZENITH, INC.

235 Cates Hill Road, Apt. 228　　　　　　　　　　603-555-0185 (home)
Berlin, NH 03570-1552　　　　　　　　　　　　　603-555-0141 (work)

## QUALIFICATIONS

| | |
|---|---|
| Experienced Sales Associate | Eight years of retail sales experience<br>Choose merchandise<br>Create eye-catching displays<br>Help customers find products to meet their needs<br>Suggest companion or comple-mentary products |
| Motivated | Promoted to Department Manager after only two years<br>Rearranged display area for improved traffic flow<br>Associate of the Month five times |
| Organized | Schedule three full- and eight part-time workers<br>Coach daughter's T-ball team<br>Worked full-time while completing degrees<br>Chaired Student Coalition child care committee (ECC)<br>Co-founder of Business Commuter Club (GMU) |
| Effective Communicator | Conduct seasonal product-use seminars<br>Trained sales associates to use POS terminal<br>Prepared flyer describing special order policy<br>Presented Child Care Center proposal to college administrative committee (ECC) |

| **EMPLOYMENT** | **EDUCATION** |
|---|---|
| Monroe Department Store | Green Mountain University, Gorham, NH |
| Hilltop Mall | Bachelor of Business Administration, May 2006 |
| Berlin, NH | Evergreen Community College, Gorham, NH |
| 1998 to present | Associate of Arts in Marketing, May 2002 |

References and Portfolio Available Upon Request

**Figure 7-4**
Solicited Functional Résumé

RAE LYNNE CONRAD
2362 Arden Drive
Sarasota, FL 34232-3861
(941) 555-0151

OBJECTIVE

A part-time receptionist position in a progressive metropolitan hospital or clinic.

EDUCATION

Chambers Business University, Bradenton, FL
Medical Secretary Program
Certificate to be awarded February 2006

Classes in Medical Terminology, Microcomputer Systems, Machine Transcription, Word
Processing, Medical Records Administration, and Business Communication.

SPECIAL SKILLS

Keyboarding; text accuracy 95 percent at 55 wpm
Keyboarding; statistics accuracy 95 percent at 25 wpm
Windows 98 - XP, Microsoft Office, WWW, html
CPR-certified

WORK EXPERIENCE

Jake's Cafe, Sarasota, FL
Hostess, Cashier, Scheduler
Server and Table Clearer

ACTIVITIES AND INTERESTS

Bradenton Community Hospital Hospice Volunteer 2000-present
CBU Business Club Secretary 2004-05
Cycling, softball, and handcrafts

REFERENCES

References may be obtained by writing or phoning:
Placement Office
Chambers Business University
4900 Elizabeth Avenue
Sarasota, FL 34233-3929
(941) 555-0189

**Figure 7-5**
Scannable Résumé

# Application Letters

An **application letter** accompanies a résumé and provides additional information about the applicant's employment qualifications. Like résumés, application letters are expected to reflect the background and personality of the job seeker. The characteristics of an application letter are as follows:

- *Application letters are brief.* Keep the letter to one page.

- *Application letters parallel résumés.* The résumé and the letter should follow the same organizational plan. If education is listed first in the résumé, it should be developed first in the letter. The letter and résumé should be worded differently. Use the letter to expand upon what was presented in the résumé.

- *Application letters refer to résumés.* The writer mentions the résumé in the text of the message and uses an enclosure notation.

- *Application letters are prepared individually.* Address the letter to the interviewer. Phone the organization to get the person's name, the correct spelling, and the title. If you are unable to identify someone to whom to address the letter, use a general title and salutation such as *Dear Human Resource Manager* or *Dear Sales Manager.*

- *Application letters are original.* The letter should be a reflection of the writer. Use books, magazines, websites, pamphlets, or messages authored by friends or relatives as guides, but do not copy them. Explain as honestly as you can why you want the specific job and how the employer will benefit from hiring you.

- *Application letters use personal pronouns.* The writer is focusing on his or her qualifications, so it is difficult not to begin every sentence with I. For variety, the writer can:

Use an introductory word, phrase, or clause to begin the sentence.
*Currently, I . . .*
*While studying accounting at Jefferson College, I . . .*
*You are seeking someone with experience, and I . . .*

Make the reader the subject of the sentence.
*As you read the enclosed résumé, Ms. Sullivan . . .*

Use qualifications as the subject of the sentence.
*Creativity and enthusiasm are among the qualifications I offer Regional Broadcasting.*

Use the passive voice.
*Practical work experience has been a valuable supplement to my academic preparation.*

The purpose of the application letter is to persuade the employer to interview the applicant. Therefore, use the AIDA plan. (See Chapter 6, pages 113–116, to review the AIDA plan.)

Application letters are persuasive messages.

**ATTENTION.** The opening should state what type of job the writer wants. When writing to a company that has a job opening, begin by saying how information about the job was obtained.

> The computer specialist position posted on your company website indicates you are seeking someone with strong technical ability and good interpersonal skills. My education and experience have helped me develop these skills and more.

When applicants are unsure of whether an opening exists, they can begin the letter with a statement or question that includes information about their qualifications.

> Organized . . . motivated . . . educated in sales techniques . . . these are some of the qualities I would bring to the staff of Becker Brothers. When you have an opening for a sales representative, adding me to your staff will increase the energy, enthusiasm, and productivity of your force.

## [THINKING IT THROUGH 7-2]

## Attracting Attention

Rewrite this letter segment to correct the problems you note.

Dear Store Manager

Last spring, you spoke to my retail management class at Wichita Technical College. I was very impressed with the information you gave us. I am now interested in a career in fashion merchandising.

**INTEREST AND DESIRE.** The attention-getting opening should provide a natural transition to the interest and desire sections of the message. Throughout the interest and desire sections of an application letter, the writer should be concerned with expanding on and providing evidence to support what is listed on the résumé.

> While employed at The Name of the Game, I had a perfect attendance record. Whenever an emergency fill-in worker or someone to stay extra hours was needed, my manager knew he could rely on me.

**ACTION.** End the message by asking the employer for an interview. Be courteous and positive. Offer to meet at the employer's convenience. Personalize the close by including the name of the reader and/or the name of the company.

> Ms. Sanchez, may we meet to discuss how my education and experience can benefit McMillan Computers? I can be reached by phone at home after 3 p.m. any weekday and can be available for an interview at your convenience.

## Letter Format

Application letters are formatted as personal-business letters. The same font and type size used for the body text of the résumé are usually used for the letter. Application letters should be printed on the same printer as the résumé, using the same size and quality of stationery. Putting an application letter on company letterhead is never acceptable. The writer's return address can be part of the signature lines or above the date. Figure 7-6 shows the information above the date.

[ **THINKING IT THROUGH 7-3** ]

## Asking for an Interview

Assume that you live in Baltimore and are applying for a job in Dallas. Write an action close that asks for an interview.

212B North Glebe Road, Apt. 33
Arlington, VA 22203-3722
April 17, 200-

Mr. Alex Billowby
Human Resource Manager
Major Publishing Company
300 D Street SW
Washington, DC 20024-4703

Dear Mr. Billowby

Your ad in the April 16 edition of the *Capital Tribune* describes the qualities you seek in an editorial assistant. I believe I possess those qualifications and wish to apply for the position.

In June I will complete requirements for a certificate in the two-year Office Technician program at Blake Business Academy. My courses have provided me with a solid background in computing and keyboarding. I am familiar with the Windows® operating system and am proficient with word processing, spreadsheet, graphics, and database software. I am able to key straight copy at 65 wpm with 95 percent accuracy. My oral and written communication skills are strong.

Practical work experience supplements my education. My part-time position at Arco Insurance as an office assistant/receptionist has given me valuable experience in setting priorities and meeting deadlines. Working with clients has enabled me to enhance my interpersonal communication skills.

The enclosed résumé provides more information about my education and work experience and describes activities in which I have been involved. My volunteer work with the Girls' Club of Arlington has been especially rewarding and has enhanced my ability to plan and to be a contributing member of a team.

Mr. Billowby, I am eager to discuss with you how my skills and abilities might be put to work as an editorial assistant at Major Publishing. I will call you next week to request an appointment, or you may reach me at (202) 555-0128. I am looking forward to meeting you.

Sincerely

*Dawn L ubinsky*

Dawn Lubinsky

Enclosure

**Figure 7-6**
Application Letter

# Proofread and Sign

Before you mail your application letter and résumé, proofread them at least twice. Have someone whose judgment you trust review the documents. Sign the letter with black ink; make sure your signature is legible. Organizations receive applications from many qualified applicants. An error, even a small one, can eliminate job seekers before they get an interview.

*Accuracy is critical.*

## Sending Résumés and Letters

An application packet can be sent by conventional mail, sent by e-mail, faxed, or delivered in person.

**CONVENTIONAL MAIL.** Place the letter on top of the résumé. Do not fold, clip, or staple the materials. Send them in a large envelope with a mailing label that includes your and the receiver's address information.

**E-MAIL.** Don't send your application as an e-mail attachment unless you first receive permission from the potential employer. Attachments are notorious for containing viruses; many receivers delete them without opening. Also, if the sender and receiver have incompatible ISPs, use different computer platforms, or operate incompatible word processing software, files may not be accessible or may look like gobbledygook.

When you plan to send a résumé and letter as text embedded in an e-mail, create the documents using a word processing program and save them as text or ASCII files. Then use a text editor such as Microsoft® WordPad to make the documents resemble your originals. Insert spaces in place of tabs, and use hard returns at the end of each line. Adjust the margins to ensure the lines contain no more than 60 characters. The plus sign can act as a bullet. An asterisk before and after an item will highlight it. The advertised job title or relevant job number makes an attention-getting subject line.

Be sure to proofread carefully. Sending the e-mail to yourself or a friend and accessing it with a different program than was used to create it is a good test of whether the format will be retained.

**FAX.** Employment application materials should be faxed only at the employer's request or to meet a deadline. You may phone the employer to verify that the materials were received. Even though you've faxed your materials, be sure to follow up with mailed originals.

**IN PERSON.** If you choose to deliver your application materials, be sure to make a good first impression. Dress professionally, and treat everyone with courtesy and respect. Ask to speak with your intended receiver (most likely someone in the human resources department), but if a receptionist offers to take the envelope, accept the offer and thank the individual.

## What Happens Next?

Several things can happen after you send your letter and résumé to a potential employer. You may receive an acknowledgment. You may be asked to complete an application form. You may be invited for an interview.

If you haven't heard anything for two weeks after the application deadline, phone or write the employer to ask about the status of your application.

> *Application forms are sometimes completed online.*

> *Some websites provide an online scroll box in which you paste your letter of application and résumé.*

> *Interview invitations are usually extended by phone.*

If an employer sends you an application form, complete and return it promptly. Read the instructions carefully. To avoid making content errors, photocopy the form and fill in all required information on the copy first. If the instructions say to handwrite your responses, do it in black ink. The space provided for responses is usually quite small; good handwriting is essential. Put a blank sheet of paper between the pages of a multi-page form before you complete it to stop images from shadowing onto other pages. When a question does not apply to you, write **N/A** (not applicable) to show the employer that you read the question. Sign your complete, legal name.

Interviewers may verify the information provided in the résumé and application letter. They will assess your ability to communicate clearly, think logically, behave professionally, and be well mannered socially. The employer will gather information about these qualities by asking questions, listening to responses, and observing the interviewee.

*Respond to all questions on an application form.*

## Portfolios

A **portfolio** is a collection of work samples that showcases an applicant's education and experience. It supplements the application letter and résumé and provides evidence of the qualifications highlighted there. The availability of a portfolio is included as a notation on a résumé or as a statement in an application letter. A potential employer might ask to view the portfolio as part of the screening process, but it is more common for the applicant to offer it during the job interview.

The contents of a portfolio and the way in which it is developed vary by applicant and employment field. Business-related portfolios may be printed and placed in an indexed binder or stored on a CD or disk. Regardless of presentation format, the portfolio should be well organized and easy to access. Some applicants organize their portfolio to match the skills identified in the job description (e.g., teamwork, computer skills). A list of items that could be included in a portfolio follows:

- Agendas of meetings you led
- Class project products
- Computer programs or applications
- Documentation of licenses
- Workshop participation certificates
- Evidence of awards and honors
- Personal philosophy or mission statement
- Positive performance evaluations
- Presentation handouts and sample slides
- Presentation outlines
- Recommendation letters
- Research papers
- Transcripts
- Writing samples

Portfolio development is a long-term project, not something to be entered into casually as one begins a job search. Collect and index materials as you prepare them. Class projects and papers can be revised and edited after they have been graded and returned to you. A portfolio is a living document; continue to refine it after you get a job, and use it as you seek promotions, transfers, or new employment. Copyrights and confidentiality concerns may prevent you from including full copies of work-related projects and presentations, but summaries that describe challenges and outcomes can be valuable portfolio additions.

## Other Employment Messages

Two additional messages deserve mention here because they relate to the job search. They are **reference requests** and **interview follow-ups**. Thank-you letters will be covered in the section on Goodwill Messages.

### Reference Requests.
Always ask permission before including the name of a reference on your résumé or an application form. When a written request is used, organize the message by the direct approach. Indicate you are seeking a particular type of employment, and ask permission to list the recipient as a reference. If the person is unfamiliar with your qualifications, explain them or enclose your résumé.

### Interview Follow-up Messages.
Within five days after an interview, send a follow-up message to the people you met. A follow-up message shows good business and social skills.

*Follow up after an interview.*

If your initial application materials were sent by e-mail or posted online, you may use e-mail for your interview follow-up message. If your initial application was mailed, do the same with your interview follow-up. Prepare the letter on the same size and quality of paper used for the application letter and résumé. Whether sent in print or electronic form, your message should be brief and organized by the direct approach.

Begin by thanking the interviewer for meeting with you. Include the date of the interview and the specific job for which you applied. In the second paragraph, remind the employer of your strongest qualifications. If the interviewer was impressed by a particular item in your background, mention it in your follow-up. If you can, provide information that will overcome any perceived weakness. Conclude the message by expressing your continued interest in the position. Figure 7-7 shows an interview follow-up e-mail.

*Courtesy is never out of style.*

### Acceptance or Rejection Letters.
Offers of employment are most often extended first orally and then in writing. The applicant's decision about the job is handled in a similar manner. Both messages are written using the direct approach—the acceptance because it is

```
┌──────────────────────────────────────────────────────────────────┐
│ ●●●                         ✉ Mail                                 │
├──────────────────────────────────────────────────────────────────┤
│ New Message  Send  Address  Attach  Options  Spelling  Print  Save │ File  Edit  Format  Insert  Tools  View  Help │
├──────────────────────────────────────────────────────────────────┤
│      To:  abillowby@majorpublishing.com                            │
│      Cc:                                                            │
│  Subject:  Editorial Assistant Position                            │
│ ▶ Attachments:                                                     │
├──────────────────────────────────────────────────────────────────┤
│                                                                    │
│  Thank you for meeting with me on Friday, May 28, to discuss the   │
│  editorial assistant position available at Major Publishing. I     │
│  appreciate the time you took to explain the job and the           │
│  qualifications you are seeking in a person to fill it.            │
│                                                                    │
│  As we discussed during the interview, my education and work       │
│  experience provide me with a solid foundation from which to begin │
│  employment. My research and proofreading skills, my proficiency   │
│  with various computer software programs, and my ability to        │
│  communicate effectively would be assets in the job.              │
│                                                                    │
│  Mr. Billowby, I am very interested in working for Major           │
│  Publishing. If I can provide additional information to convince   │
│  you that I'd be a productive editorial assistant, please let me   │
│  know. If another interview would be useful, I'll be happy to come │
│  at your convenience. I look forward to hearing from you and to    │
│  the possibility of joining the editorial staff.                   │
│                                                                    │
│  Dawn Lubinsky                                                     │
│  212B North Glebe Road, Apt. 33                                    │
│  Arlington, VA 22203-3722                                          │
│  (202) 555-0128                                                    │
│                                                                    │
└──────────────────────────────────────────────────────────────────┘
```

## Figure 7-7
Interview Follow-up E-mail

good news and the rejection because the bad news would already have been presented orally. Both messages should be positive and should create goodwill between the sender and the receiver. The acceptance letter can focus on the challenge of the job and the writer's enthusiasm for joining the company. The rejection letter can contain positive statements about the interview process and the people involved in it.

RESIGNATION LETTERS.   When an employee decides to leave a company, he or she will generally convey the news to the manager or supervisor in person. Good business practice dictates, however, that the resignation also be submitted in writing and retained in the employee's employment file. The message should open with the resignation and indicate the last date of employment.

The remainder of this brief message should be positive or neutral and should focus on some aspect of the work experience. Writers need not describe their future plans. They definitely should not make derogatory comments about the work or other employees; such comments reflect poorly on the writer and may adversely affect future business dealings with the employer or with others who currently work for the organization.

# GOODWILL MESSAGES

It is always good business practice to take advantage of opportunities to be courteous to clients and colleagues. **Goodwill messages** are sent to thank, apologize, congratulate, offer sympathy, invite, welcome, or extend special greetings.

The sole purpose of a goodwill message is to make the reader feel good about an event, accomplishment, or award that he or she has received. Attempts to sell products or promote services can cheapen or defeat this purpose.

Goodwill messages can be handwritten, printed, or sent electronically. The formality of the message varies with the occasion and with the relationship between the sender and receiver. Suppose that a businessperson extends sympathy to a coworker whose spouse recently died. Because of the intensely personal nature of the event, the sender would probably buy a sympathy card and add a handwritten message to it. If the event were a fire that destroyed a local television station, the writer might send a letter. A congratulatory message could be sent electronically using one of the many Internet postcard sites.

Whatever the situation and whatever the relationship between the sender and the receiver, goodwill messages are written using the direct approach and are sent as soon as possible after learning of the event or accomplishment. The following paragraphs contain suggestions for writing specific types of goodwill messages.

© 1997 Ted Goff

## Appreciation

The first paragraph should contain a sincere expression of gratitude and should state specifically why thanks are being extended. The middle section of the message should expand on some impressive or especially meaningful part of the situation. Gratitude can be expressed again in the close, but the wording should be different than that used to open the message. When writing a thank-you note to someone who was an employment reference for you, include a few details about the job.

Vary your word choice when expressing gratitude.

## [ THINKING IT THROUGH 7-4 ]

### Saying Thanks

When Taylor Tower opened a luggage store in the Harbor Mall, he received a large floral arrangement from the mall manager. Write three sentences that Taylor could use to express thanks for the arrangement. Use different wording in each.

## Apology

The key to writing an apology is to tell your reader what action you are taking to prevent a repeat of the situation. Begin with an apology, describe remedial actions, and close with a positive statement about the future.

## Congratulations

Begin by extending good wishes and stating why you are congratulating the reader. Say why the reader is worthy to have received the specific award or honor. End positively. If the message is to begin and end with a congratulatory statement, vary the wording. Figure 7-8 on the next page illustrates a congratulatory message.

" *Gratitude is the most exquisite form of courtesy.* "

**-Jacques Maritain**

**Life House**

August 4, 200-

Mr. Harvey Ridenouer
18 Harris Avenue
Jamaica Plain, MA 02130-2848

Dear Harvey

Congratulations!

Being selected Jamaica Plain's *Volunteer of the Year* is an honor you truly deserve. Your years as a member of the LifeHouse Board of Directors and the leadership you showed during last year's fundraising drive illustrate your commitment to providing a safe, friendly refuge for troubled teens. The successful matching grant proposal you wrote was the key that opened the door on the Teen Center project.

Harvey, LifeHouse is privileged to have you as a member of its family. You're a terri c role model for the youth we serve.

Sincerely

*Jennifer Gliniany*

Jennifer Gliniany
Director

dg

275 Centre Street | Jamaica Plain, Ma 02130-1640 | (617) 555-0183

## Figure 7-8
Congratulatory Message

# Sympathy

*Choose words that comfort the reader.*

State your feelings early in the message. If you can and are willing to be of assistance, say so. Specific offers of help are more meaningful than general offers of assistance. End by looking positively to the future.

# Invitation

*Pay attention to details.*

Begin by naming the event the receiver is being asked to attend. Indicate whether a guest is permitted. Those who receive the invitation will come from a variety of family situations, so phrase the invitation to apply to all readers. Include all details the receiver needs to decide whether to attend—day, date, time, place, and cost. The reader might appreciate knowing whether formal, business, or casual clothing should be worn. If a reply is desired, say how, to whom, and by when. Encouraging the reader to accept the invitation is one way to end the message positively. The message should be warm and friendly.

## Welcome

Welcome messages can be sent to new employees, new clients, or new residents of a community. Start with a warm expression of welcome, and then explain why the association will be mutually beneficial. End with another expression of welcome, or build positively on some aspect of the new relationship.

## Special Greetings

Birthdays, weddings, anniversaries, births, and holidays are some of the special occasions that call for goodwill messages. Begin by extending greetings, add a personal statement about the event, and end positively.

---

### [THINKING IT THROUGH 7-5]

## Recognizing Special Occasions

You are administrative assistant to the human resource manager of a large clothing manufacturing firm located in Los Angeles, California. The men and women you employ range in age from 16 to 70. Some are U.S. citizens; some come from other countries and have permits to work in the United States. It's December 1, and your supervisor is considering sending a Christmas message to the plant's employees.

On a separate sheet of paper, write the advice you would give your supervisor about the appropriateness of sending such a message.

---

## MINUTES OF A MEETING

Minutes provide historical and practical documentation of reports, important discussions, decisions, and announcements made during meetings. Formal minutes follow the guidelines of a parliamentary authority such as *Robert's Rules of Order*. Informal minutes follow the practice of the group or the preference of the recorder. Meeting minutes usually include the following:

- Group name
- Time meeting begins and ends
- Names of leader, participants, and guests
- Action(s) taken on minutes of previous meeting(s)
- Report summaries
- Summaries of important discussions
- Follow-up assignments
- Announcements
- Name and signature of person who recorded the minutes

Events are reported in chronological order. Motions and their results are reported exactly as stated during the meeting. The minutes are presented attractively, with side headings used to guide the reader. When distributed promptly after a meeting, minutes help in planning the agenda for

> Minutes provide a practical and historical record.

the next meeting and remind participants of tasks for which they are responsible. Figure 7-9 shows an example of minutes.

---

## Staff Council Meeting
### November 10, 200-, 2 p.m., Room 272
### Minutes

**Presiding:**    M. Provost

**Participants:**    B. Aldof, G. Gunderson, T. Hardy, C. Rios, C. Unger (Guest)

Minutes of the November 4 meeting were approved as distributed.

### Reports

- The worker satisfaction survey is ready for distribution. Some concern about distributing it so close to the holiday season. Moved/Seconded/Passed: The survey will be distributed as scheduled.

- G. Unger described the status of negotiations with the company's insurance carrier. Health care costs continue to rise. Additional information will be available at the next meeting.

### Old Business

- Security. Facilities Department is reviewing our proposal that combination locks be installed on first- and second-floor restroom doors. Marked for follow-up in six weeks if no response is received.

### New Business

- Retirement Planning Seminar. Discussion about possibility of sponsoring one for workers. B. Aldof will investigate speakers and costs.

### Announcements

Next meeting November 17. Meeting adjourned at 2:35 p.m.

*Walter Ellington*

Walter Ellington, Recorder

---

**Figure 7-9**
Meeting Minutes

# NEWS RELEASES

*News releases are sent to print, radio, and television outlets.*

Organizations use news releases to announce good news, put a positive slant on bad news, and reassure the public in times of crisis. Figure 7-10 shows a news release. Follow these guidelines when preparing a news release to be sent to representatives of the print and electronic media:

- Place the date of the release and the name and phone number of the organization's contact near the top of the first page.
- Put the name of the city from which the release originates at the beginning of the first paragraph.
- Use an attention-getting opening, called a **lead**, that briefly states what the news is.
- Answer *who? what? when? where? why?* and *how?* in a sequence that puts the most important items first. If editors and announcers are short of space or time, they will cut text from the end.

### KAMIKA INTERNATIONAL
**104 E. Baraga Ave.**
**Marquette, MI 49855-4738**

[1] **(906) 555-0177**                    **(906) 555-0178 FAX**

**NEWS RELEASE**          [2] **Contact Person:** Marv Carter
[3] September 3, 200-
**For Release:** Immediately

**DENISE RAU NAMED CHIEF EXECUTIVE OFFICER**
**OF KAMIKA INTERNATIONAL**

[4]    MARQUETTE, MI—Denise Rau has been named Chief Executive Officer of Kamika International, the region's leading producer of cold-weather footwear.

Rau joined Kamika in 1988 after earning her BS degree in Finance from Jackson University. Since then, she has held a variety of posts, most recently Executive Vice President.

In announcing the appointment, Kamika's Board Chairman, Edwin Somerset, said, "Denise has the energy and ideas to propel Kamika into the future. Her experience and her commitment to the company and the people of this region make her an outstanding choice for this important role."

Rau is active in Leadership Marquette, serves on the symphony board, and volunteers with the hospice at County General Hospital. She resides in Marquette with her husband, Fred, and their three children.

[5] ###

**Annotations**

[1] Phone number of contact person

[2] Name of contact person

[3] Date

[4] City from which release originates

[5] Shows end of release

**Figure 7-10**
News Release

- Use short sentences and simple words.
- Double-space the text. Put -MORE - at the bottom of every page that is to be continued, and center ### or - 30 - below the last line of the release.

The competition for column inches and airtime is great. Writers can increase the chances of having their releases selected for print or broadcast by addressing their copy to a specific editor or program manager and by writing for the particular print or broadcast audience the receiver represents.

# CHAPTER SUMMARY

- Employment communication involves both written and oral communication.
- A résumé is a description of an applicant's qualifications for employment.
- Résumés include some or all of the following parts: an opening; sections about education, work or other experience, special skills, activities and interests; and a statement about references.
- Résumés can be organized using a reverse chronological, functional, or combination approach and formatted as a traditional paper, scannable, or online résumé.
- An application letter accompanies a résumé and provides additional information about the applicant's employment qualifications.
- Application letters follow the AIDA plan for persuasive messages and are formatted as personal-business letters.
- Proofreading of résumés and application letters is essential. A typographical error can eliminate an applicant from consideration.
- A portfolio is a collection of work samples that showcases an applicant's education and experience.
- Other employment-related messages are reference requests, interview follow-up messages, thank-you letters, acceptance and rejection letters, and resignation letters.
- Goodwill messages are used to bring social warmth to the business environment; their sole purpose is to make the reader feel good.
- Appreciation, apology, congratulations, sympathy, invitation, welcome, and special greetings are types of goodwill messages.
- Goodwill messages are organized by the direct approach.
- Minutes provide a historical and practical record of what happened at a meeting.
- News releases attract the attention of the media and are used by organizations to announce good news, present bad news positively, and manage a crisis.

# SU

An Equal Opportunity Employer
**SOUTHWESTERN UTILITIES**
2900 E. Shea Boulevard   Phoenix, AZ 85028-3207

# APPLICATION FOR EMPLOYMENT

## PERSONAL INFORMATION *(Please print clearly.)*

Name _____   Soc. Sec. # _____
First                         Middle                          Last

Address _____
Street                     City                    State                   ZIP

Phone _____   Have you worked for SU before? ☐ Yes  ☐ No   When? _____

## AVAILABILITY

Are you legally able to be employed in this country?   ☐ Yes   ☐ No   (if hired, verification will be required by law)

Position desired _____   Date available _____

Would you accept part-time employment? ☐ Yes  ☐ No   Temporary employment? ☐ Yes  ☐ No

Other positions for which you are qualified _____

Location preference or restrictions _____

Why are you seeking a job change? _____

Starting salary desired _____

## EMPLOYMENT *(List most recent jobs first.)*

Company_____   Street Address _____

City_____   State_____ ZIP_____   Telephone_____

Position_____   Supervisor_____   May we contact? ☐ Yes  ☐ No

Dates employed: From _____ To _____   Reason for leaving _____

Wage_____   Duties _____

Company_____   Street Address _____

City_____   State_____ ZIP_____   Telephone_____

Position_____   Supervisor_____   May we contact? ☐ Yes  ☐ No

Dates employed: From _____ To _____   Reason for leaving _____

Wage_____   Duties _____

Company_____   Street Address _____

City_____   State_____ ZIP_____   Telephone_____

Position_____   Supervisor_____   May we contact? ☐ Yes  ☐ No

Dates employed: From _____ To _____   Reason for leaving _____

Wage_____   Duties _____

## U.S. MILITARY SERVICE

Branch of Service _____   From _____ To _____

Highest rank or grade _____   Major duties _____

_____

## EDUCATION AND TRAINING

**High School** _____ Street Address _____

City _____ State _____ ZIP _____ From _____ To _____

Did you graduate? ☐ Yes ☐ No    If no, highest grade completed _____ Grade avg. _____

**College** _____ Street Address _____

City _____ State _____ ZIP _____ From _____ To _____

Major _____ Diploma/degree/certificate _____ Grade avg. _____

**Graduate School** _____ Street Address _____

City _____ State _____ ZIP _____ From _____ To _____

Major _____ Diploma/degree/certificate _____ Grade avg. _____

**Voc/Bus/Trade School** _____ Street Address _____

City _____ State _____ ZIP _____ From _____ To _____

Major _____ Diploma/degree/certificate _____ Grade avg. _____

Special skills, licenses, certificates, etc. _____
_____

## PERSONAL

Have you had any convictions other than minor traffic?    ☐ Yes ☐ No    If yes, what and when? _____
_____

## REFERENCES _(List three persons not related to you whom you have known for at least one year.)_

Name _____ Street Address _____

City _____ State _____ ZIP _____ Telephone _____

Position _____ Years known _____

Name _____ Street Address _____

City _____ State _____ ZIP _____ Telephone _____

Position _____ Years known _____

Name _____ Street Address _____

City _____ State _____ ZIP _____ Telephone _____

Position _____ Years known _____

## IMPORTANT: READ BEFORE SIGNING

The facts set forth in my application are true and complete. I understand that false statements on this application shall be considered cause for refusal of or separation from employment. I authorize investigation of all statements and matters contained in this application that Southwestern Utilities may deem relevant to my employment. I authorize all my previous employers or other persons having information concerning me to provide such information to Southwestern Utilities. I release Southwestern Utilities and any person providing information to Southwestern Utilities from all claims or liabilities whatsoever in connection with making such investigations or disclosures.

I understand that Southwestern Utilities makes no promise or agreement to employ me for a certain period of time. If I am employed, Southwestern Utilities may terminate my employment at any time, with or without cause, for any lawful reason.

Signature of Applicant _____ Date _____

1. Find an employment ad or announcement that interests you in your local paper or on the Internet. Prepare a résumé that you can use to apply for the job. Attach a copy of the ad or announcement to your résumé when you submit it to your instructor. Keep the original ad or announcement for use in Application 3.

2. Convert the résumé prepared in Application 1 to scannable format.

3. Using the ad or announcement you found for Application 1, prepare a letter of application that responds to it.

4. Select a company for which you would like to work. Assume that you don't know whether the company has an opening. Prepare an appropriate letter of application.

5. As your instructor directs, use your résumé to help you complete the application form on pages 161–162. The form is also posted in the Supplemental Activities section of *The Basics: Business Communication* website at http://www.merrier.swlearning.com.

6. Select a former employer and prepare a letter asking permission to list the person as a reference.

7. Select a current faculty member and prepare an e-mail asking permission to list him or her as a reference. Send the message to your instructor.

8. Two weeks have passed since the deadline to apply for the position in Application 3; write a follow-up message.

9. Assume that you were interviewed for a job. Prepare a follow-up letter to send to the interviewer.

10. You've been hired for the job! Write to thank one of the people in Application 6 or 7 who gave you a reference.

11. It's 2 p.m. Friday. You returned to your office after taking notes at a luncheon meeting of the planning committee, a meeting that should have ended at 1:15 pm. You check your desk calendar and realize you missed your 1:30 appointment with Ed Duff, employee benefit specialist in the HR Department. Ed wanted to leave the office at noon but stayed because you wanted to meet with him. You phone his office and learn that he has left. The appointment can be rescheduled, but you feel you owe Ed an apology for missing the meeting. You decide to send him (your instructor) an e-mail.

12. One of the pleasures of being employed by Vicom Publishers is working with Ashley Rickert. Ashley is a friendly, optimistic young woman who loves life and thoroughly enjoys the creativity her position as graphic artist offers her. You and Ashley met at the new employee orientation session and have been friends ever since. Your friendship extends beyond the confines of the office; she and her husband, Mark, frequently socialize with you and your (spouse or date). Last Saturday, Ashley and Mark told you they are expecting twins!

   a. You've purchased a card to send to Ashley and Mark. Handwrite a personal note to include in the card.

*continued on next page* ▼

b. Ashley has been told to spend the final month of her pregnancy at home and eliminate all physical activity; visitors are prohibited. Compose an uplifting letter to send her. Ashley's address is 13404 Morning Glory Drive, Lakeside, CA 92040-4752.

c. Ashley's delivery was very difficult; one of the babies did not survive. You've purchased a sympathy card. Write a personal message to include in the card.

13. Your local Chamber of Commerce recently selected two of your colleagues, Mary Ylinen and Todd Westholm, to receive its Ambassador Award, which recognizes contributions to the community. Mary is an old friend. You grew up in the same neighborhood and were classmates in high school. She is supervisor of your company's travel department and is very active in Mothers Against Drunk Driving. Todd joined your firm three years ago. He supervises the office services division. You were both part of a cost-cutting task force last year. He is a volunteer with the American Cancer Society. Write messages congratulating Mary and Todd.

14. You manage the apartment building in which you live. During the past week, residents have been evacuated four times due to a short in the fire alarm system. Two of those evacuations occurred between midnight and 6 a.m., and one occurred during a thunderstorm. The problem has been fixed, but the building owner has asked you to write an apology that can be slid beneath each resident's door. Do so.

15. You operate a travel agency. You recently learned that the space next to you has been leased to Margo Kelpel, who plans to operate a sunglasses store. Prepare a message to welcome her to the mall.

16. It's February 16, and you're happy. You can credit just one thing for your cheerful spirit: the school play you saw last night. It was delightful—due in great part, you believe, to the performance given by your eight-year-old niece, Madeleine. Despite Madeleine's incredible talent, you realize that the teacher also played a part in the play's success. Write a letter to your niece's teacher to acknowledge his contribution to the success of the show (Mr. Tony Miller, Merriwood Academy, 182 Brookdale Road, Stamford, CT 06903-4116).

17. As department head, prepare an e-mail inviting members of your six-person department to a barbecue at your home a week from Saturday.

18. Attend a meeting at your school or in your community. Record minutes for the event.

19. Prepare a news release announcing the recall of the Model CC backpack. The thread used to stitch the seams is weak and could break, causing users to lose the contents of their pack. Your company is Better Trails, Inc., 300 Idaho Street, Elko, NV 89801-3136, 800-555-0140, 775-555-0144 (fax). List yourself as the contact.

20. Prepare a news release announcing your election as student representative to your school's governing board. List Paul Blair as the contact.

## BUSINESS LETTER
### Block Style

**FRIENDS AND NEIGHBORS**
516 W. Iowa Street
Dermott, AR 71638-2039
(870) 555-0183                                                    Letterhead

December 7, 200-     **About 2 inches or two lines below letterhead.**     Date

↓ 4

Mr. Alex P. Perkla                                               Letter
Homemade Construction                                           Address
571 S. Pecan Street
Dermott, AR 71638-2225

↓ 2

Dear Mr. Perkla                                                 Salutation

↓ 2

Thank you for helping to make this year's Friends and Neighbors     Body
dinner a success.

The tables and benches your crews built, delivered, and set up
were put to good use. Meals were enjoyed by 376 people who
might otherwise have spent their holiday alone and hungry.

Homemade Construction has a positive reputation in the
community. That reputation is well deserved.

↓ 2

Sincerely                                                      Complimentary
                                                               Close

↓ 4

Chuck L. Fosgate, Chair                                        Signature
                                                               Lines
↓ 2

vu                                                             Reference
                                                               Initials
↓ 2

c     Chamber of Commerce                                      Copy Notation

# BUSINESS LETTER

## Simplified Style

| | |
|---|---|
| Letterhead | **FRIENDS AND NEIGHBORS**<br>516 W. Iowa Street<br>Dermott, AR 71638-2039<br>(870) 555-0183 |
| Date | December 7, 200-   **About 2 inches or two lines below letterhead.** |
| | ↓ 4 |
| Letter<br>Address | Mr Alex P. Perkla<br>Homemade Construction<br>571 S. Pecan Street<br>Dermott, AR 71638-2225 |
| | ↓ 2 |
| Subject Line | Holiday Gratitude |
| | ↓ 2 |
| Body | Thank you for helping to make this year's Friends and Neighbors dinner a success.<br><br>The tables and benches your crews built, delivered, and set up were put to good use. Meals were enjoyed by 376 people who might otherwise have spent their holiday alone and hungry.<br><br>Homemade Construction has a positive reputation in the community. That reputation is well deserved. |
| Signature<br>Lines | ↓ 4<br><br>Chuck L. Fosgate, Chair |
| Reference<br>Initials | ↓ 2<br>vu |
| Enclosure<br>Notation | ↓ 2<br>Enclosures |

# HEADING FOR SECOND AND ADDITIONAL PAGES OF LETTERS AND MEMOS

↓ **About 1 inch**

Mr. Alex P. Perkla
Page 2  (use appropriate page number)
December 7, 200-
↓ 2
Body of message is continued. At least two lines of text should be carried to continuation pages.

# PERSONAL-BUSINESS LETTER

## Modified Block Style

**About 2 inches**

143 W. Mulberry Street
Dermott, AR 71638-1200
December 7, 200-

↓ 4

Mr. Alex P. Perkla
Homemade Construction
571 S. Pecan Street
Dermott, AR 71638-2225

↓ 2

Dear Mr. Perkla

↓ 2

Thank you for helping to make this year's Friends and Neighbors dinner a success.

The tables and benches your crews built, delivered, and set up were put to good use. Meals were enjoyed by 376 people who might otherwise have spent their holiday alone and hungry.

Homemade Construction has a positive reputation in the community. That reputation is well deserved.

↓ 2

Sincerely

↓ 4

Chuck L. Fosgate, Chair
Friends and Neighbors Dinner

↓ 2

Enclosures

**Return Address**
**Date**

**Letter Address**

**Salutation**

**Body**

**Signature Lines**

**Enclosure Notation**

# TRADITIONAL MEMO

**About 2 inches**

**Memo Headings**

**TO:**  Marketing Department Staff
↓ 2
**FROM:**  Paula Pierz, Manager  *pp*
↓ 2
**DATE:**  September 25, 200-
↓ 2
**SUBJECT:**  Staff Meeting
↓ 2

**Body**

Representatives of ACE Computer Corporation will be here October 7, 8, and 9 to conduct training sessions for us. These all-day sessions will be held in Conference Room A; equipment will be installed there for our use. Please bring the following materials with you:

**Treat bulleted items as paragraphs.**

- Operating system manual.

- Graphics software manual.

- Word processing software manual.

**Align text for readability.**

- Samples of letters, memos, reports, and proposals you have completed during the past six months.

The attached brochure will more fully describe the training we will receive. Please read it before the first session.

These classes will provide a good introduction to our equipment and software. It is important that we all attend. Sessions covering advanced applications will be scheduled after the first of the year.
↓ 2

**Reference Initials Attachment Notation**

eb
↓ 2
Attachment

# ADDRESSING AN ENVELOPE

Business and personal-business letters are usually mailed in No. 10 envelopes (4 1/8″ × 9 1/2″), but personal-business letters can also be mailed in No. 6 3/4 envelopes (3 5/8″ × 6 1/2″).

Business envelopes typically have the return address preprinted; therefore, return addresses are keyed only for personal-business letters or when a letterhead envelope is not available. You can use the envelope feature of your word processing program to create the mailing address and, if necessary, the return address for these and other envelope sizes. As you do so, remember these guidelines:

- An address must contain at least three lines; addresses of more than six lines should be avoided.

- The last line of an address must contain the city, the state, and the ZIP Code (preferably the nine-digit code).

- Mailing addresses may use title case or be keyed in uppercase with no punctuation.

- Place mailing notations that affect postage (e.g., CERTIFIED or REGISTERED) below the stamp position.

- Place other notations (e.g., CONFIDENTIAL or PERSONAL) below the return address.

# FOLDING AND INSERTING CORRESPONDENCE

Large envelopes (No. 10)

| Step 1 | Step 2 | Step 3 |
|---|---|---|

 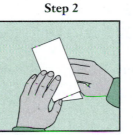 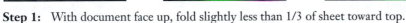

**Step 1:** With document face up, fold slightly less than 1/3 of sheet toward top.
**Step 2:** Fold top of sheet to within 1/2″ of bottom fold.
**Step 3:** Insert document into envelope with last crease toward bottom of envelope.

Small envelopes (No. 6 3/4)

| Step 1 | Step 2 | Step 3 |
|---|---|---|

 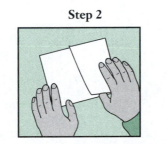 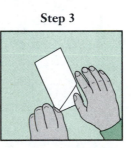

**Step 1:** With document face up, fold bottom up to 1/2″ from top.
**Step 2:** Fold right third to left.
**Step 3:** Fold left third to 1/2″ from last crease and insert last creased edge first.

| Symbol | Meaning | Before | After |
|---|---|---|---|
| ◡ | Close | can not | cannot |
| ℓ | Delete | the the day | the day |
| ℰ | Delete and close up | oather | other |
| ... or stet | Don't change | simple plan | simple plan |
| ¶ | Paragraph | Please let me know when when you plan to arrive. I look forward to seeing you again. | Please let me know when you plan to arrive. I look forward to seeing you again. |
| no ¶ | No new paragraph | Please let me know when you plan to arrive. I will meet your flight. | Please let me know when you plan to arrive. I will meet your flight. |
| ∧ | Insert | at that time | at that time |
| ⊙ | Insert period | Gina ended the meeting | Gina ended the meeting. |
| ∧ | Insert comma | In the first place | In the first place, |
| ∨ | Insert apostrophe | cant | can't |
| ⊏ ⊐ | Move left or right | 27.16  11.12 | 27.16  11.12 |
| ↱ | Move copy | That digital camera only costs $59.95. | That digital camera costs only $59.95. |
| ∽ | Transpose | to quickly go | to go quickly |
| ≡ or cap | Capitalize | joe | Joe |
| lc or / | Lowercase | Manager | manager |
| ○ sp | Spell out | Oct. | October |
| / # | Insert space | once again | once again |
| — | Italics | A Man for All Seasons | *A Man for All Seasons* |
| ∼∼ | Bold | Paragraph 1. | **Paragraph 1.** |

# Frequently Confused/ Misused Words

| | |
|---|---|
| accept | to receive |
| except | other than |
| | |
| advice | words of help |
| advise | to give advice or counsel |
| | |
| affect | to influence |
| effect | outcome or result; to bring about |
| | |
| already | before the expected time |
| all ready | fully prepared |
| | |
| alternate | a substitute; to change repeatedly from one to another |
| alternative | a choice between or among things or actions |
| | |
| among | used with three or more persons or things |
| between | used with two persons or things |
| | |
| anyone | any person |
| any one | any one of many persons or things |
| | |
| anytime | no particular time (**not** preceded by *at*) |
| any time | no particular time (preceded by *at*); any amount of time |
| | |
| anyway | in any case |
| any way | by any manner |
| | |
| as | relating to (conjunction that introduces a clause) |
| like | similar to (preposition, followed by a noun or pronoun) |
| | |
| assure | to promise or guarantee |
| ensure | to make certain |
| insure | to protect life or property from loss |
| | |
| badly | describes how a person or thing acts or behaves |
| bad | describes how a person or thing is (use *bad* in conjunction with the five senses—touch, taste, smell, sight, and sound) |
| | |
| beside | next to |
| besides | in addition to |
| | |
| both | two items or people considered together |
| each | any number of items or people considered separately |
| | |
| bring | to carry to the speaker or the speaker's place |
| take | to carry away from the speaker or the speaker's place |

| | |
|---|---|
| can | able to do something |
| may | permission; possibility |
| capital | chief or main; city that serves as the seat of government of a state or nation; an uppercase letter; a sum of money or wealth; a form of punishment |
| capitol | building used by a congress or state legislature |
| come | move toward the speaker or the speaker's place |
| go | move away from the speaker or the speaker's place |
| everyday | routine; common |
| every day | each day |
| everyone | everybody |
| every one | each one |
| farther | physical distance |
| further | additional |
| fewer | a smaller quantity or amount (used with plural nouns and things that can be counted) |
| less | a smaller amount or degree (used with singular nouns and things that cannot be counted) |
| good | skillful; admirable; having the right qualities (adjective) |
| well | properly; with skill; in a kindly way (adverb); healthy (adjective) |
| imply | to hint or suggest |
| infer | to conclude or determine |
| in | location; position |
| into | motion from one place to another |
| irregardless | Not a word; do not use. |
| regardless | in spite of |
| its | possessive form of *it* |
| it's | contraction meaning "it is" |
| lead | metallic element |
| led | past tense of *lead* |
| lose | opposite of *win* |
| loose | not tight or not secure; free |
| past | at a time gone by |
| passed | moved beyond; circulated |
| personal | private |
| personnel | workers; employees |
| precede | to come before |
| proceed | to continue; to go forward |

| | |
|---|---|
| principal | main; chief; head of school; sum of money |
| principle | guide; rule |
| raise | to lift something or cause it to rise (requires an object) |
| rise | to get up or move upward (does not take an object) |
| real | true or actual (used to describe a noun or pronoun) |
| really | truly or actually (used with verbs, adverbs, or adjectives) |
| than | as compared to |
| then | at that time |
| their | possessive pronoun |
| there | at that place |
| they're | contraction for "they are" |
| to | toward; for the purpose of |
| too | also; excessive |
| two | the number 2 |
| weather | atmospheric conditions, such as rain |
| whether | introduces one of two possibilities or choices |
| who's | contraction of "who is" |
| whose | shows ownership or possession |
| you're | contraction for "you are" |
| your | possessive pronoun |

# Thinking it Through Solutions

## CHAPTER 1

### Thinking it Through 1-1

Responses will vary with your work situation. Perhaps you cited the importance of receiving clear, accurate instructions from your supervisor. Or, you may have mentioned the importance of communication among members of your work team. Another possibility is in-person, telephone, or written communication with customers.

### Thinking it Through 1-2

Hopefully, you will disagree. Although examples of unethical behavior may receive publicity, the vast majority of business transactions and the people who complete them are ethical.

### Thinking it Through 1-3

Your response should describe a situation in which time is a major factor or one in which emotional or confidential content is involved. Both face-to-face and telephone communication facilitate speedy delivery and feedback.

## CHAPTER 2

### Thinking it Through 2-1

1. **General Goal(s):** To inform; to persuade.
   **Specific Goal:** To provide details of the meeting and show it is a worthwhile investment for the company, not merely an opportunity to visit a desirable location.
2. **General Goal(s):** To inform.
   **Specific Goal:** To provide data necessary to make decisions about how to improve air quality.

3. **General Goal(s):** To inquire.
   **Specific Goal:** To obtain information about a regulation so that your organization may comply with it.

4. **General Goal(s):** To inform; to persuade.
   **Specific Goal:** To provide information about current and proposed operations; to persuade the lending agency to approve the loan.

5. **General Goal(s):** To persuade.
   **Specific Goal:** To convince the claim representative to reverse his or her decision and pay the claim.

## Thinking it Through 2-2

Responses will vary. Education could affect the individual's knowledge of the tax system and the seriousness of an audit. Every individual should be interested in avoiding penalties and having to pay additional taxes.

## Thinking it Through 2-3

1. To inform.
2. To tell the patient the records have been sent; maintain goodwill.
3. Verbal (written).
4. Letter.
5. Direct.
6. B should be first; A should be last. The remaining items could be arranged in various ways.
7. To inform; to persuade.
8. To retain the receiver and members of the receiver's family as patients of the clinic.
9. Business letter.
10. Traditional mail.
11. Direct. The physician's retirement is the main idea.

# CHAPTER 3

## Thinking it Through 3-1

1. Sample responses:

   a. yield, give in, surrender
   b. quick, prompt, efficient

   c. flawless, perfect, spotless

   d. combination, coincidence, union

   e. practical, realistic, useful

2. Sample responses:

   a. 750 rpm

   b. in 30 minutes

   c. 2 inches tall

   d. in 5 minutes

   e. give this your lowest priority

## Thinking it Through 3-2

Answers will vary. You could use several types of transitions in your paragraph(s):

- Additional information: entry-level and long-term career goals
- Cause and effect: Because I am studying X, I will pursue a career in Y.
- Contrast: Although I have studied X, I want to do Y.
- Sequence: First, I will . . .; then, I will . . .
- Time: Before entering school, I . . .; now, I . . .

## Thinking it Through 3-3

Answers may vary slightly

1. While waiting for the bus, I saw a limousine stop in front of the hotel.
2. Before locking the door, the guard set the alarm.
3. As I approached the conference room, I heard people laughing and clapping.
4. Hardware and finances limit the amount of programming the television station can offer.
5. Correct.
6. Dylan was impressed by and appreciative of Rosalee's remarks.

## Thinking it Through 3-4

Answers may vary slightly.

1. In order to take advantage of the offer, you need to know how many items of each type are available, the size, and the style (e.g., two-drawer lateral file). You might also want information about color. It would also be important to know whether the items are free; if not, you need to know the price of each item.

2. You could get most of the information you need with a reply e-mail or phone call. You would probably make a personal visit and see the equipment to get all the information you need.

3. A phone call is probably the quickest, most efficient method. If James doesn't answer, you could leave a voice-mail message for him. E-mail is another option. Depending on how many messages James receives, however, your message may not get immediate attention. In addition, the message could get long because you have several questions to pose.

## Thinking it Through 3-5

Sample response:

Reference manuals are resources for those who write or prepare business messages. Writers may view reference manuals as style guides or "how to" books. Most manuals contain information about grammar, punctuation, capitalization, abbreviations, word division, numbers, symbols, and proofreading. Some also have sections on topics such as technology, filing, and getting a job.

## Thinking it Through 3-6

Answers may vary slightly.

1. Users can access their personal account at any time.
2. Nurses should submit their continuing education certificates to their supervisor.
3. Someone left a cell phone in the computer lab.
4. Most businesspeople would probably favor the plan.
5. Mechanics should keep their tools in good condition.
6. Anyone can find his or her way around the campus.

# CHAPTER 4

## Thinking it Through 4-1

Responses will vary.

1. A vertical list helps readers:
   a. Focus their attention on what the writer thinks is important.
   b. Organize their responses, if a reply is needed.
   c. Find particular items if they need to refer to the message more than once.
   d. Follow directions or instructions.

2. A vertical list helps writers:

   a. Draw attention to specific items in a message.
   b. Be sure all important items have been included.
   c. Make it easier for the reader to respond.
   d. Present directions or instructions in an organized way.

## Thinking it Through 4-2

Sample response: Please send a Model 1126 MP3 player to replace the one that arrived in damaged condition.

## Thinking it Through 4-3

Advise Jordan to describe the problem calmly and clearly and to furnish documentation of his purchase. He might also ask for instructions on how to return the damaged player.

## Thinking it Through 4-4

Sample response: Because the player is a gift for my sister's birthday, I would appreciate receiving a replacement unit by June 12.

## Thinking it Through 4-5

1. The message should thank the customer for ordering, explain the order is being processed, and give an indication of when merchandise will be shipped. The invoice for the purchase could be included as part of the message.

2. Thank you for shopping with us. Your order for the items listed below is being processed and will be shipped within three business days.

   You may track your order online. Simply access our home page, link to "Shipping Information," and enter (tracking number) when asked for your tracking number. We value your business and look forward to meeting your sporting goods needs again in the near future.

(order information)

# CHAPTER 5

## Thinking it Through 5-1

1. Weak. It doesn't introduce the topic of the message.
2. Weak. It is condescending and gives the bad news before the explanation.

3. Weak. It avoids the topic of the message.
4. Weak. The reader might believe the repairs will be free.

## Thinking it Through 5-2

1. Receivers benefit by continuing to have high-quality cleaning while helping to protect the environment.
2. Receivers benefit because they know the company is concerned about protecting its clients from theft and respects their right to privacy.

## Thinking it Through 5-3

Responses will vary. Sample responses:

*Implied Bad News:* Our 15 percent quantity discount is available only on purchases of 50 or more figurines.

*Expressed Bad News:* In order to qualify for our 15 percent quantity discount, you must order 50 or more figurines. Therefore, your order for 10 figurines will be processed at our regular low price.

*Choice and Explanation:* The implied bad news is softer and, therefore, preferred in a message to this new customer. The message could express confidence that the figurines will sell well and that Marie's future orders will qualify for the discount.

## Thinking it Through 5-4

1. Weak. It suggests the problem will occur again.
2. Strong. It refers to a counterproposal and makes action easy.
3. Weak. It doesn't relate to the topic of the message.
4. Weak. It refers to the bad news.

## Thinking it Through 5-5

Sample response: Pam, you have every reason to believe your performance review will be positive. Your work reflects skill and creativity.

(The close might be "I'm looking forward to meeting with you in July.")

## Thinking it Through 5-6

Responses will vary. Sample responses:

1. The reader would probably react positively. He or she could expect that an adjustment will be made because the problem was caused by a manufacturing problem rather than a use problem.
2. The reaction could be neutral because the subject line doesn't say whether an adjustment will be made.

3. The reader would probably react neutrally. The subject line refers to the topic without giving a clue about whether the claim will be adjusted.

4. The reaction would probably be positive; the subject line leads the reader to believe an adjustment will be made.

5. The reaction would probably be negative; the subject line indicates that the request for replacement won't be honored.

# CHAPTER 6

## Thinking it Through 6-1

1. Responses will vary. Sample responses:

   a. life insurance/new parent—security (provide financial security), money (for college)

   b. changing location of supply cabinet/office supervisor—convenience and efficiency (more centrally located, more room to access contents)

   c. magazine subscription/senior citizen—intelligence (general knowledge), enjoyment (foster hobby or interest area)

   d. ergonomic chair/office worker—comfort and good health (improve posture, reduce fatigue)

   e. tax preparation/sales associate—time and money (time savings, accuracy, familiarity with current law)

2. Sample response for b: Productivity can be increased by moving the supply cabinet to the west wall, adjacent to the file cabinets.

## Thinking it Through 6-2

1. Number of people who attended last year's show.
   Number of people who stopped at your booth.
   Number of new customers generated as a result of displaying at the show.
   Dollars of revenue generated from new customer accounts.

2. Compare the revenue generated from this event with the revenue generated from other forms of advertising. Remind your supervisor that the larger space will allow you to display more of your products. You could also offer to eliminate another less productive form of advertising.

3. No. In fact, you might ask for a response well before the registration deadline to be sure the company gets a prime location.

## Thinking it Through 6-3

Responses will vary. Sample responses:

| | |
|---|---|
| Title: | Safety First |
| Problem Statement: | During the past six months, 4 of our 17 warehouse clerks have missed two or more days of work due to on-the-job injuries. |
| Objective: | To reduce the number of job-related injuries among warehouse workers by at least 25 percent in the next six months. |
| Methods/ Activities: | Classify injuries to determine whether a pattern exists. |
| | Consult the National Institute for Occupational Safety and Health (NIOSH) website for advice. |
| | Institute a safety suggestion system within the warehouse. |
| | Review equipment operation and safety precautions with workers. |
| | Post "safety first" signs on equipment and throughout the warehouse. |
| | Establish an incentive plan to reward the warehouse team for consecutive days without injury. |
| Evaluation: | Review attendance and injury report data in six months. Based on those data, determine which methods/activities should be continued. Consider surveying workers to get their input on which activities were most effective. |

# CHAPTER 7

## Thinking it Through 7-1

Responses for the second and third questions will vary.

1. The objective is weak because it is so general.
2. The objective is strong. It mentions the type of position desired and the type of institution in which the applicant wishes to work. It also specifies the geographic location and shows ambition.
3. The objective is fairly strong. It mentions the type of position desired and some of the skills the applicant would bring to the position. Mentioning advancement would strengthen, but lengthen, the objective.

### Thinking it Through 7-2

The first problem with this illustration is that it isn't directed to a specific person. If the writer doesn't remember the speaker's name, he or she should get the information from the retail management class instructor. The second problem is that the paragraph isn't specific. What is it the receiver seeks?

Sample response:

Dear Mrs. Wilson

Your presentation to WTC's retail management class last spring inspired me to pursue a career in fashion merchandising, and an internship at The Petite Lady would be an excellent start. Please accept this letter as my application for such a position.

### Thinking it Through 7-3

Sample response:

Mr. Crawford, I will be in the Dallas area the first week of March and would appreciate the opportunity to meet with you then. I look forward to discussing the marketing position with you.

### Thinking it Through 7-4

Sample response:

Thank you for the beautiful floral arrangement that was delivered this morning!

How thoughtful it was for you to recognize the opening of my store with a lovely spring bouquet.

My customers, staff, and I genuinely appreciate the colorful bouquet you delivered this morning.

### Thinking it Through 7-5

Not all workers celebrate the Christmas season; therefore, you could advise your employer to send a Happy New Year message or one with an end-of-year good wishes theme. A Christmas message phrased as an invitation to share the sprit of the season with those who celebrate it might also be appropriate.

# INDEX